Knit It Now!

Turn Great Yarns into Great Sweaters

Julie Montanari

Knit It Now!

Turn Great Yarns into Great Sweaters

Martingale®
& COMPANY

Dedication

I dedicate this book to all those that teach and inspire us. In particular:

Mathilda Montanari, my grandmother; she spoke little English and I spoke less Italian, but somehow she taught me how to move the needles and create the magic.

Dorothy Lohman, a neighbor and friend; she taught me to follow a pattern and opened up a new world of knitting possibilities.

Helen Montanari, my sister; her own work took my breath away and always inspired me to do a better job.

Acknowledgments

Special thanks to the amazing owners and staff at all the great yarn shops in the world; in particular, Kim McFall and Ann Gevas from Fengari in Half Moon Bay, Roxanne Seabright from Artfibers in San Francisco, and the staff of the button counter at Britex Fabrics in San Francisco.

My heartfelt appreciation goes to all those at Martingale & Company, whose talent and hard work turned this project into a reality.

Credits

PRESIDENT • *Nancy J. Martin*
CEO • *Daniel J. Martin*
PUBLISHER • *Jane Hamada*
EDITORIAL DIRECTOR • *Mary V. Green*
MANAGING EDITOR • *Tina Cook*
TECHNICAL EDITOR • *Ursula Reikes*
COPY EDITOR • *Liz McGehee*
DESIGN DIRECTOR • *Stan Green*
ILLUSTRATORS • *Robin Strobel, Laurel Strand*
COVER DESIGNER • *Stan Green*
TEXT DESIGNER • *Trina Stahl*
PHOTOGRAPHER • *Brent Kane*

& COMPANY

Knit It Now! Turn Great Yarns into Great Sweaters
© 2004 by Julie Montanari

Martingale & Company®
20205 144th Avenue NE
Woodinville, WA 98072-8478 USA
www.martingale-pub.com

Printed in China
09 08 07 06 05 04   8 7 6 5 4 3 2 1

Mission Statement

Dedicated to providing quality products and service to inspire creativity.

Library of Congress Cataloging-in-Publication Data

Montanari, Julie.
    Knit it now! : turn great yarns into great sweaters / Julie Montanari.
        p.   cm.
Includes bibliographical references.
    ISBN 1-56477-559-3
1. Knitting—Patterns. 2. Sweaters. I. Title.
TT825.M66 2004
746.43'20432—dc22

2003027117

Contents

Introduction

I love yarn. I buy too much yarn. That is, I buy yarn much faster than I can knit sweaters. I buy yarn because it's beautiful, because I love the color, or because I love the feel of it. I love imagining what it will be like to knit. When I buy yarn, I only have a vague idea of what I may do with it or what style sweater I may want to make. Then I take a wild guess at how much yarn I'll need and come home with it. As you can imagine, I have a cabinet that is full to bursting with amazing yarns. It is this cabinet that inspired this book.

One day, I took inventory. I made a list of all the beautiful yarns in the cabinet. There were several cottons with interesting textures, a couple of gorgeous cashmere blends, a great textured chunky wool, a soft mohair ribbon, a huge felted merino, and one-of-a-kind silks. The colors took my breath away. Some were bright, some were rich, and some were subtle. Many were variegated; a few were hand dyed. And, of course, there were lots of leftovers—one or two or three balls from previous projects. You name it, I had it.

As much as I loved admiring the cabinet full of yarn, I wished I were looking at a closet filled with beautiful sweaters made from those amazing yarns instead! I estimated that it could take me a year or more to turn these beautiful yarns into beautiful sweaters. But what a fun year it would be!

So I stopped buying and started knitting. (Well, I didn't completely stop buying, but I slowed down a lot!) One at a time, I started playing with the yarns. I tried different needle sizes and different stitch patterns until I found one that really brought out the best in each particular yarn. These yarns tended to be wrong for complicated patterns; they had so much going on within them that detailed patterns would get lost. But they did scream out for great textures.

When I found a stitch pattern that was great with one yarn, I tried it on a few different yarns. A few stitch patterns emerged that worked wonders with my collection of amazing yarns; they were flexible enough to bring out the great qualities of a wide variety of yarns. These are the six stitch patterns that are featured in this book. They are each demonstrated with both solid and variegated yarns, lightweight and heavier-weight yarns, as well as casual and dressy yarns. For each stitch pattern, I have one or two sweaters that are a simple execution of the stitch. Then I've added a couple more patterns that demonstrate some other ways to play with the stitch.

As a collection, this book represents a wardrobe of sweaters for all seasons. There are several little warm-weather shells, a few winter pullovers, cropped shapes for in between, and enough cardigans to go around. There are a few glittery pieces, others businesslike, and some right for a walk in the woods. There are a wide variety of necklines and sleeve lengths.

None of the patterns in this book is fussy. All the stitch patterns are simple enough to become routine within a couple of pattern repeats. Similarly, all the sweaters are simple, classic shapes. Several are good beginner projects. When knit in fairly bulky yarns, a few become quick one- or two-weekend projects.

Don't worry about using the specific yarns shown in this book. These yarns are the ones I have purchased over the last few years from a variety of stores. Some are still available and some are not. Wonderful new yarns come out every day. There is no "right" yarn for any of these patterns. Experiment with different weights and textures, solid and variegated yarns, and a variety of needle sizes. To help your imagination, I have included samples of how different yarns look in the same project. Each pattern includes directions for a range of stitch gauges. The result is the ability to customize these patterns for a wide variety of beautiful yarns. The choices are yours.

I hope that you will use these patterns as a point of departure. Use the yarns that you have fallen in love with! So, is there some yarn in your closet? Something you've fallen in love with at the yarn store? Let's start knitting!

Making a Great Sweater That Fits!

For each of the sweaters in this book, I have described the project in the following steps. This is the plan that I believe will give you the best sweater—one you'll love and one that fits!

Before You Begin—Fall in Love!

Find a yarn that you love and a sweater design that looks right for it. Making a good match between pattern and yarn is somewhat of an art. There are few general guidelines. For example, a smooth, light-colored yarn will show off pattern detail the best; that is, you'll be able to see every stitch in detail. But that same pattern may also be beautiful in a fuzzier yarn that softens the look a bit. I love the look of a fine bouclé in a lace pattern, or a fuzzy mohair yarn in an intricate pattern. Variegated yarns are wonderful in some stitches. Some detailed cable stitches look great in black. So, treat this as a creative process and explore. Remember that even an "easy" or "quick" project is a major investment of time and money. Don't bother with a project you're not excited about.

Step 1: Play with Your Yarn

This is the official first step of each sweater pattern. Do not skip it! I have heard knitters say they hate to bother with a gauge swatch;

I've never understood that. For me, this first chance to work with a new yarn is the most exciting time. Have fun with it!

The knitting directions in each chapter begin with the stitch patterns used for the sweaters. All directions in this book include selvage stitches. Selvage stitches are the first and last stitch in each row. They are outside of the pattern work and are knit on both the right-side and wrong-side rows. They are shown in the directions with the symbol "KS." The selvage stitch will provide a neat edge that will make seaming easier.

To begin, make a swatch using the yarn and stitch pattern you're planning for the

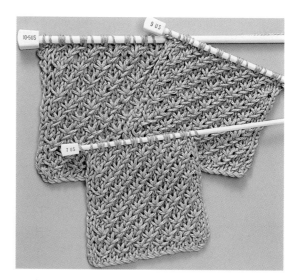

Different needle sizes will create different-weight fabric from the same yarn. One might be right for a soft, flowing cardigan and one for a warm jacket. Choose the weight that's right for your project.

body of the sweater. Start with your best guess of the right needle size for this project. Remember that needle sizes will vary, depending on the yarn, the stitch, and the weight of the fabric you want to create. Plan on making your swatch at least 5" wide and 4" long.

First question: Do you like the weight of the fabric? If the fabric seems too dense, stiff, or warm, try again with bigger needles. Alternately, if it's too floppy or sheer, try it with smaller needles. There is no right answer here, only personal preference. The patterns in this book all allow for a range of stitch gauges. Choose the fabric you like best.

Second question: Is this the right project for this yarn? Does the stitch highlight the great qualities of the yarn? Do you find the stitch comfortable to knit? You may want to explore different stitch patterns for your yarn. Or change yarns; many yarn stores will let you return unopened skeins of yarn within a reasonable time period.

When you're ready to commit, go back to your swatch. Bind it off. (Check the "Tips" box for the stitch you're using. Some have recommendations for binding off the stitch.) Let the swatch relax to its natural tension; that is, the tension you want the fabric to have when you wear it. For a rib pattern with a lot of scrunch, natural tension might mean slightly stretched. Using straight pins, mark the center 4" of width in the middle of the piece.

Measure across a full 4" in the center of the fabric, away from edge stitches.

Count the stitches between the pins. Measure a second time in a different spot to double-check your count. The difference of only one stitch in your gauge measure will change the finished size of the sweater by 2" to 4". *Getting an accurate stitch gauge is the single most important step in making your sweater fit.*

At this time, you will also want to take a look at the cast-on and bind-off rows of the swatch. Do they stretch enough? Do they lie flat? Compared to the body of the swatch, do they pull in or stretch out? You can use smaller or larger needles for either or both of these rows, or experiment with different techniques if necessary.

If the sweater has a contrast trim—a second yarn or second stitch used for button bands or other trim—you will need to make a second gauge swatch for the trim. Cast on about 5" of stitches and work the trim pattern for the width you will use for the actual trim (usually 1" or 2"). Check that the weight of the fabric is appropriate; I usually want fairly dense fabric for the trim. Bind it off, the way you would for the actual sweater. Make sure that your bind-off row lies flat and even. Check whether you need to use larger or smaller needles for the bind off, or work at a different tension. When the bind-off row is straight and flat, then measure your stitch gauge. Keep a note of the trim gauge and the needle size you used for the work and for the bind-off row.

While I'm exploring different needle sizes, I usually unravel my experimental gauge swatches and reuse the yarn. Once I have a final gauge swatch, I keep it. I include it with the notes I keep on all the sweaters I make. Saving the swatch means that I start the sweater with fresh, unused yarn. Some yarns can be happily reused a couple times before they start to show wear, but some cannot. For example, delicate ribbon yarns and lightweight mohair yarns are much prettier the first time they are used. So, I prefer to start with fresh yarn when I start knitting for real.

Step 2: Find the Right Sweater Size and Pattern Number

First, ask yourself what sweater size you want. Think about it carefully. Here is a general guideline: The fit of the sweater is determined by the difference between your bust measurement and the actual finished measurement of the sweater—the "ease" of the sweater.

- A tight sweater is made up to 2" smaller than your bust measurement.
- A fitted pullover or shell is made equal to or up to 2" larger than your bust measurement.
- A roomy, but not baggy pullover is 2" to 4" larger than your bust measurement.
- A vest or roomy cardigan is 4" to 6" larger than your bust measurement.
- An oversized fit is 6", or more, larger than your bust measurement.

Remember that individuals have very different preferences about how they want their sweaters to fit. Also note that bulky-weight yarns need more "ease" to give the same fit.

If you are not sure what size to make, I recommend that you measure a favorite sweater to use as a reference. Find a sweater *of similar weight fabric* as a guide. With luck, you'll have a sweater in the closet that fits just right. If necessary, go to the store and find one that fits right. Now measure this sweater across the chest, just below the underarm seam. This is the "finished sweater size" you want to make.

Next you need to determine what pattern number will produce the sweater size that you want. The directions for each sweater are presented in five pattern numbers: 1, 2, 3, 4, and 5. The pattern number alone does not tell you what size your sweater will be—it is the combination of pattern number and stitch gauge that determines your sweater size. For example, if you are working in the chunky gauge range and your stitch gauge is

14 stitches over 4", a pattern number 3 will produce a 33" sweater. If your gauge is 11 stitches over 4", that same pattern number 3 will produce a 44" sweater! You must use the gauge range tables on pages 11 and 12 to determine the pattern number that will produce the sweater size that you want.

To find the correct pattern number to use, follow these steps:

1. Find the table on pages 11 and 12 that corresponds to the gauge range for your sweater pattern. For example, if you want to make the Banded Shell, you will notice on page 22 that this pattern is designed for the "Worsted Gauge range," which means that your gauge must fall between 15 and 20 stitches over 4".

NOTE: *Gauges 10, 15, and 20 each appear in two ranges; for example, 10 sts over 4" appears in both Super-Chunky Gauge and Chunky Gauge ranges. Make sure you are using the table for the correct range! Quickly double check the caption underneath the model sweater for your project.*

2. Go back to your gauge swatch; measure carefully and determine the number of stitches over 4".

3. Find the column in the table that corresponds to your stitch gauge. Read down the column until you reach the row that matches the finished sweater size that you want. The number where these two values intersect (stitch gauge and sweater size) is the pattern number you should use. For example, if you want to make the Banded Shell, and your gauge is 19 stitches over 4", go to the fifth column in the Worsted Gauge range table. If you want to make a size 40" sweater, go to the row for a 40" sweater size. The number where these two values intersect is 4. This will be the pattern number that you follow in the directions.

The number of stitches to make for this pattern number will always appear in the

Super-Chunky Gauge Range

Needle Size: Approx 11–17

Finished Sweater Size	Gauge (No. of sts to 4")		
	8	9	10
	Pattern Numbers		
33"		1	2
36"	1	2	3
40"	2	3	4
44"	3	4	5
48"	4	5	

Chunky Gauge Range

Needle Size: Approx 9–11

Finished Sweater Size	Gauge (No. of sts to 4")					
	10	11	12	13	14	15
	Pattern Numbers					
33"			1	2	3	3
36"		1	2	3	4*	4
40"	1	2	3	4	4*	5
44"	2	3	4	5	5	
48"	3	4	5			

*At a gauge of 14 sts = 4", pattern size 4 will produce a finished sweater size of approx 38".

Worsted Gauge Range

Needle Size: Approx 7–9

Finished Sweater Size	Gauge (No. of sts to 4")					
	15	16	17	18	19	20
	Pattern Numbers					
33"		1	1	2	2	3
36"	1	2	2	3	3	4
40"	2	3	3	4	4	5
44"	3	4	4	5	5	
48"	4	5	5			

DK Gauge Range
Needle Size: Approx 5–7

Finished Sweater Size	Gauge (No. of sts to 4")					
	20	21	22	23	24	25
	Pattern Numbers					
33"		1	1	1	2	2
36"	1	2*	2	2	3	3
40"	2	2*	3	3	4	4
44"	3	3	4	4	5	5
48"	4	4	5	5		

*At a gauge of 21 sts = 4", pattern size 2 will produce a finished sweater size of approx 38".

changes for pattern numbers 2, 3, 4, and 5 following in parentheses: 1 (2, 3, 4, 5). In our Banded Shell same position in a series. Directions for pattern number 1 are listed initially, with sweater example, your pattern number is 4, so you would always use the number in the "4" position above. For instance, if the directions say "BO 5 (5, 5, 7, 7) sts," the number in the 4 position is 7, so you would bind off 7 stitches. When you see only one number, it applies to all pattern numbers.

4. As you proceed with your pattern, always keep your stitch gauge, your sweater size, and your pattern number in mind. You may want to go through and circle all the correct pattern numbers before you begin working. Refer to the Sweater Measurements chart (in each project's directions) to determine the back length, front length, and so forth, for the garment you are making. If your finished sweater size is 40", follow the measurements in the column below 40".

Note: If you are aiming for an "average" size sweater of 36" or 40", you can work in any of the gauges shown in the range for your sweater. If you want to make a smaller size, you'll need to be at the higher end of the gauge range (thinner yarn and smaller needles). For a larger sweater, you'll need to be at the lower end (bulky yarn and larger needles). It is likely that you would use different pattern numbers for different projects.

Step 3: Gather Your Materials

Once you've determined the stitch gauge and pattern number, you can determine how much yarn you will need for your project. Each pattern includes a table indicating the required yardage. The numbers in the yardage tables are designed to be generous. Still, you may want to get an extra couple of balls or skeins before you start. Think of these extra balls as project insurance. They will give you more flexibility to make your pieces longer or to reknit sections. If you end up not using them, many yarn stores will let you return unused yarn within a reasonable amount of time. If you're like me and sometimes use yarn a couple of years (decades?) after you buy it, look at these extras as a resource. They are great for scarves, sweater trims, and striped patterns.

Let me add a disclaimer here about mohair. I find that projects made in mohair take about one-third less yarn than the same size project in other fibers. But none of the patterns here were designed for specific fibers. Even if the model sweater is shown in mohair, the yardage charts will indicate enough yarn for (hopefully) any fiber you choose. When you work with mohair, you may have a lot of yarn left over.

By this point, you will have determined the needle size you want to work with, so the patterns don't specify a needle size. The descriptions of the featured sweaters do indicate the yarn and needles used to create the models shown.

For patterns with pick-up-and-knit button or neckbands, I suggest a **crochet hook** to make this easier. If the neckband is long (such as the continuous band of a V-neck cardigan), you'll need to use a **long circular needle** to hold all the stitches. A few patterns require a **cable needle.** In addition, I assume you have the following basic tools:

+ tape measure
+ scissors
+ stitch holders for holding stitches to be worked later
+ stitch markers
+ safety pins for pinning sweater pieces together
+ tapestry needles for sewing pieces together
+ spare yarn to use for basting
+ calculator

Step 4: Review Your Sweater Measurements

Each pattern includes diagrams of the sweater pieces you will be making. Key measurements are drawn in and labeled A, B, C, etc. Below each diagram is a table that indicates the length of these measurements for the finished sweater size you will be creating. Refer to the values for your finished sweater size, regardless of your pattern number. For example, if you are making a 40" sweater size, follow the measurements in the column below 40".

The knitting directions refer to the value in this table; for example, "at measurement C, beg armhole shaping as follows. . . ." Simply use the value from the table for the given measurement (in your size) as you proceed with the next block of directions.

Take a look at these measurements before you start knitting. Feel free to adjust these to your personal taste. Sweaters can be lengthened or shortened easily by increasing or decreasing the length below the armhole. Pay attention to whether the pattern has straight side seams. If there are decreases between the bottom of the sweater and the armhole, space them properly for your adjusted length. If you're lengthening sweaters, think about whether the sweater width at the bottom will be sufficient at the longer length. You may need to add some side shaping or choose a larger size. Make sure you have enough yarn.

Changing the length from the armhole to the neck is trickier. For a sleeveless shell, this measurement is critical to the fit of the sweater. Too long, and there won't be enough coverage in the underarm. Too short, and . . . ouch! Think about this measurement carefully. Remember to consider the effect of the finish at the armhole. Some patterns have armhole bands that are 1" or more wide; some have thin crocheted trim. If the sweater has sleeves, then changes in this length on the front and back pieces must correspond to changes in the sleeve cap (see "Step 9").

Sleeve lengths can also be adjusted, but wait until step 7 to make this decision.

Step 5: It's Time for the Real Thing: Knit the Back First

Unless otherwise specified, make the back first. All sweaters in this book are knit from the bottom up. Check the width early. After a few inches of knitting, stop midway through a row (or at the end of a row if you're using circular needles) and spread the sweater out to its full width. If your needles aren't long enough to spread the sweater to its full width, then mark the center of the sweater piece and spread one half of the piece out fully. For a rib pattern, stretch the fabric slightly until it looks like you want it to look when you're wearing it. Make sure that the sweater is coming out the width that you expected. Even with the best gauge swatch, we've all been fooled when we knit a full width. If the piece is significantly different than you meant it to be, start over; you won't regret it. Re-measure your gauge (using the sweater beginning piece), and choose the pattern size that will generate the right sweater size.

You should also double-check at this time that your cast-on row has the right amount of stretch. If not, you'll need to start over with a different cast-on method or a larger needle for the cast-on row.

When it's time to measure the length, stop in the middle of the row, spread the piece to full width, and hold it up. As a general rule, you should expect a piece to stretch a bit vertically, so err on the side of making your piece a little shorter than you want, rather than longer. This is especially true when you're working on narrow areas, like shoulders. You may want to work a little tighter through the shoulder section, or even switch to smaller needles.

To get a true read on the length of your sweater, spread it out to full width and hold it up!

Step 6: Make the Front

When the back is done, make the front, matching the length of the back. I literally count rows to make sure the front and back match. (This is where stitch markers come in handy.) For cardigans, I recommend knitting the two front halves at the same time, using two balls of yarn. It will help you create two front sections that are exactly the same length. I also find it easier to keep track of the right and left side shaping when both pieces are on the needles at the same time. This may not work for very bulky projects unless you use a longer circular needle.

With both cardigan fronts on the needles together, it's easy to keep track of the shaping for the right and left sides

Step 7: Stop Here and Try It On

Baste the front and back together at the shoulders and side seams. Use a loose stitch with a contrasting yarn that will be easy to remove later. Try on your unfinished masterpiece. This is the time to make sure you are still going to love it.

Is the sweater too tight? To make a sweater wider, knit (in pattern) two narrow strips the same length as the sweater back from the bottom to the armhole. Sew these strips between the front and back pieces on the side. This really does look okay—I've done it several times. If the piece is too tight at the bottom, but fits well through the bust, make your inserts a few inches wider at the bottom, and decrease stitches as you go up. You will end up with a knitted piece that looks like a tall triangle. Insert it into the side seam the same way. Your sweater now has a slight A-line. Great!

Do the armholes fit right? Pay special attention here. Armholes often come out longer than they were intended as the knitted fabric stretches through the narrow shoulder areas.

✦ For a sleeveless sweater, look at the armhole and mentally add the width of any knitted bands or crocheted trim that will be added later. The finished sweater should fit close to your actual underarm. In particular, you want to make sure that your sweater provides enough coverage.

✦ A vest should give you enough room for the shirts and tops you will be wearing underneath. Try it on over the type of shirt you will wear with it.

✦ For a sweater that will have sleeves, the depth of the armhole should correspond to the fit of the sweater. A sweater that is fitted through the bust will have fitted sleeves, and the armhole should fall only an inch or so below your actual underarm. For a sweater with a looser fit and looser sleeves, the armhole should fall 2" to 4" lower.

If the armholes are too long, take out the neck and shoulder shaping and start them sooner. If they are too tight, start the neck and shoulder shaping later. Note that if you make the armholes a different length than specified in the pattern, then you will need to make some adjustments to the sleeves to make them fit properly.

When you are happy with the fit of your sweater, this is the time to decide about blocking. Some people swear by it. Some never do it. I do it only on fabrics that do not lie flat otherwise. That usually means mohair and wool yarns that do not have rib stitches in them. If you choose to block, do the front and back pieces now. (For more information on blocking, see page 136.)

Step 8: Finish the Neck **Now**

I mean it. This is the best way to get the sleeves right. Why? Because the right length for the sleeves depends on where the shoulder actually falls. It can be hard to predict in advance where the shoulder will fall, and guessing wrong can make a big difference in the right length and shape of the sleeve.

Follow your pattern directions for finishing the neck; the order of sewing the shoulder seams and finishing button bands and/or neckbands vary.

A few words here about pick-up-and-knit bands. For several of the patterns, the directions do not specify a precise number of stitches to pick up. The right number of stitches for a pick-up-and-knit band will depend on the gauge for the yarn, the stitch pattern, and the needles that you're using for the trim. The directions will tell you the length the band needs to be. Always confirm this measurement! Multiply by your trim gauge (expressed as stitches per inch) to determine the number of stitches to pick up. It is not important to hit this number exactly. It is more important that the trim has the right contour and lies flat.

I recommend using a crochet hook to pick up stitches and put them on your knitting needle. Using a circular knitting needle will help you visualize the shape of the bands. Just lay the sweater flat, let the needle fall along the line of the band, and reach through the fabric with the crochet hook to pick up stitches and put them on the needle.

The most critical point of a pick-up-and-knit band is the bind-off row. The tension of this row will determine how the band will lie, and therefore, how the sweater will fit. Remember that you can tighten a bind-off row after it's complete, but you can't loosen it. If you're unsure about the right tension, make the bind-off row a little loose and

It is easiest to visualize your pick-up-and-knit bands if you use a circular needle and a crochet hook.

tighten it until you're happy with the look (see "Tightening a Bind-Off Row," page 133).

For sweaters with two separate button bands, make the button side first (conventionally, the left side on a women's sweater). On the finished band, mark the locations for buttons. I usually don't buy the actual buttons until the sweater is done; I just mark the locations with safety pins. If there is no neckband above the button band, place the top button within two stitches of the top. If there will be a neckband, you probably want your top button in the neckband. Placement of the lowest button is a matter of personal choice. On long cardigans, I often place the lowest button 4" to 6" from the bottom. On shorter or hip-length cardigans, especially those with hip bands, I usually place the lowest button a few stitches from the bottom or centered within the hip band. Look at the photographs to get a feel for different options.

Space the buttons according to your personal taste. On sweaters where you want to feature the buttons, try using a lot of buttons spaced close together, or try several groups of three buttons. For other sweaters, choose subtle buttons spaced farther apart to move the focus to the fabric. Now, make the buttonhole side, matching buttonholes to button placements.

Note that there are a few patterns for V-neck vests and cardigans where the button band and neckband is one single, long, continuous band. (I recommend the longest circular needle you can find for these bands.) In this type of band, the buttonhole side and the button side are made at the same time. Make the buttonholes when the band is at one-half of its final width.

One more time, try on your close-to-finished masterpiece. Admire yourself at length. But before you take off your almost-done sweater, decide how long to make the sleeves.

Step 9: Make Sleeves That Fit

Sleeves are funny-looking things. Many sweater patterns avoid the issue of shaping sleeves by using "dropped shoulder" styling. With dropped shoulders, the front and back pieces have straight sides with no stitch reductions to create armholes. The corresponding sleeve is completely flat on top. This may be easier to knit, but it does not flatter many sweater styles. The straight armhole seam (joining the sleeve to the shoulder) falls several inches down the arm. It makes for droopy-looking shoulders and a lot of excess fabric under the arm. This book includes only one dropped-shoulder pattern, in a sweatshirt-styled sweater. There are a couple of tailored, raglan-sleeve patterns. The remainder use fitted, set-in sleeves.

A fitted sleeve generally begins with a narrow cuff, which then expands to the full sleeve width at the underarm and is topped with a bell-shaped sleeve cap. (If you have a background in sewing, you will be familiar with this shape.) The front and back pieces have armhole shaping—a curved shape that reduces the width of the sweater by several inches above the armhole. For a neat armhole seam, the final outline of the sleeve cap should be the same length or slightly longer (up to 1" or 2") than the circumference of the armhole. Note that the two pieces will curve in opposite directions— one convex and one concave.

The total outline of the sleeve cap should be the same length or a little longer than the armhole.

The goal for your sleeves is twofold: One, that the sleeve fits you well. Two, that the sleeve fits the armhole well. Let's worry about you first. To get the right fit for a set-in sleeve, you need a few key measurements. Confirm these measurements before you knit the sleeves. Try on your incomplete sweater (completed through step 8).

✦ **Sleeve length to underarm:** Pin one end of a tape measure to the bottom of the sweater armhole at the side seam. Let the underarm of the sweater fall naturally; this will be an inch or two away from the body unless it is a tight or fitted style. Hold your arm to the side at about 30°. With your palm facing down, let the tape measure run down the center of your palm and up between your fingers. The tape measure should track where the sleeve seam will be. Mark where you want the sleeve to end by putting a rubber band around your arm or wrist at this point.

Measure the length from the armhole to this rubber band.

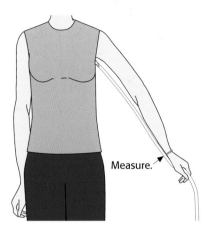

✦ **Total length of sleeve:** Pin the tape measure to the shoulder seam of the sweater. Hold your arm out at about 30°, with the other end of the tape measure between your fingers. Measure the length from the shoulder to the same rubber band used above.

✦ **Length of sleeve cap:** The length of the sleeve cap is the difference between the sleeve length to underarm and the total sleeve length. Because of the stretch of knit fabrics, a knitted sleeve cap can be 1" or 2" shorter than this measurement.

✦ **Sleeve width at bottom:** Make a loop with your tape measure of the size specified in the pattern as the sleeve width at the bottom. Place it around your arm where you put your rubber band. Check that this width seems right, considering the fit of the sweater.

✦ **Sleeve width at underarm:** Similarly, make a loop that corresponds to the sleeve width at the underarm and hold it around your arm, attached to the bottom of the underarm of the sweater. Check that it feels right.

If you just want longer or shorter sleeves, change the sleeve length to underarm. This is easy. *If you need to make the sleeve wider,* add the appropriate number of stitches to the cast-on row (an even multiple of the pattern repeat), and keep the extra stitches all the way until the final bind-off row. When you sew in the sleeve, you may have a slightly more gathered sleeve. If you prefer to avoid the gathering, make the sleeve cap 1" shorter for every 1" wider you make the sleeve. *For any other changes,* keep the geometry of the sleeve in mind. Make sure that the outline of the sleeve cap will be 1" or 2" longer than the armhole of the sweater (back plus front). To estimate the outline of the sleeve cap, add the width of the sleeve at the underarm and the length of the sleeve cap. This will give you a rough approximation.

With these measurements, knit the sleeves. Like cardigan front sections, I always make the two sleeves at the same time, using two balls of yarn. Make sure that your cast-on row will have enough stretch to comfortably pass over your hand. This is especially important if you like to roll or push up your sleeves. Check this after a few inches of knitting. Most directions specify a number of increases from the bottom of the sleeve to the armhole. Space these increases evenly over the length of the sleeve. Shape your sleeve cap as directed. Make sure there is plenty of give in the outside stitches of the cap. Block your sleeves if you have blocked the other sweater pieces.

Now let's worry about the marriage of sleeve and armhole. Using safety pins, pin the sleeves to the armholes. Pin the middle of the sleeve cap to the shoulder seam. Pin the outside edges of the sleeve cap to the outside edges of the armhole. Compare the outline of the sleeve cap to the armhole. If the outline of the sleeve cap is the same or a little longer than the armhole, great.

If the sleeve cap seems too small, check the stitches around the edges. If they were bound off more loosely, would the cap fit better? Sometimes, the fabric gets tight through decrease rows. See if the cap can be reknit with looser (and therefore longer) edges. Alternately, you can make the sleeve cap taller (1" of increased height in the sleeve cap will make the outline of the sleeve cap about 1" longer.)

Pin the sleeve in place and sew from the shoulder seam out to the edges.

When the armhole and sleeve cap match, sew the armhole seam, distributing the extra fullness in the sleeve throughout the seam. Sew, beginning at the shoulder seam and working outward. Finish the side and sleeve seams next. (If you sew, you will note that this is a different order than you would normally use in sewing.) Begin at the bottom of each seam and work in toward the underarm. For bulky fabrics, use flat seams whenever possible (see "Flat Seams," page 137). Otherwise, your seams will be very bulky and this will make your sweater feel smaller.

Alternate Step 9: Finish the Armholes

For sleeveless sweaters, this is the time for pick-up-and-knit armhole bands or crocheted edges. (See "Crocheted Edges," page 140, if you are unfamiliar with these techniques.) As with other bands, I anticipate that you may choose to make these in a contrast yarn.

As noted earlier, some patterns do not specify the number of stitches to pick up for armbands.

Rather, the directions give the circumference of the armhole (please verify!). Multiply by the gauge of your trim stitch to determine the number of stitches to pick up. It's not important to hit this number exactly; within a few stitches is fine.

After trying on the sweater, you should have an idea of how wide you want to make the armbands. Feel free to make them wider or narrower than specified in the pattern.

Remember that a fitted armband gets smaller in circumference with each row. For each ¼" of width, the armband needs to be about 1" shorter. If you are making your armbands wider than specified in the pattern, continue to decrease the number of stitches with each right-side row.

As noted with other bands, the bind-off row is the most critical point of the band. Make sure you bind off with the right tension to make the band lie flat. Err on the side of making the tension a little loose—you can tighten it up afterward (see "Tightening a Bind-Off Row," page 133). If it's too tight, you'll need to take it out and start over.

If you're making a crocheted edge, remember that the finished edge should be slightly smaller than the armhole; don't pack in too many stitches. If the final band doesn't provide as much coverage as you want, you can make a second round (with a few less stitches than the first). Alternately, choose a different crochet stitch that will provide more width to the band.

Step 10: Don't Forget the Last Little Details

+ **Reinforce any seams that need it.** I usually reinforce shoulder seams. I sometimes run a chain stitch through knit-in-place button bands if the fabric is light. If a neckline is a little loose, you can stabilize it with fabric binding.
+ **Find great buttons.** I choose buttons after the sweater and, in particular, the button-

holes are complete—I never have any luck making buttonholes match buttons. This is a place to splurge; great buttons make a beautiful sweater a work of art.

+ **Reinforce buttonholes.** If they need it, run a buttonhole stitch around your buttonholes (see page 135). This will make the edges firmer, can make too-big buttonholes a little smaller, and will keep the knitted yarns from fraying and unraveling with heavy use.
+ **Embellish.** Add beads, sequins, embroidery—go nuts!
+ **Work in all those yarn ends.**

Summary of 10 Steps to a Sweater You'll Love

1. Find a yarn you love and make an accurate gauge swatch. If your sweater has trim in a different yarn or a different stitch, make a swatch for the trim as well.

2. Identify the pattern number that will produce the sweater size you want. Forget your "usual size." *The right pattern size depends on your stitch gauge!*

3. Make sure you have plenty of yarn and any other materials you'll need.

4. Review the measurements for your sweater.

5. Start knitting the sweater back. Confirm your stitch gauge after a few inches.

6. Make the front, matching the length of the back.

7. Baste your sweater together and try it on. Check the fit.

8. Finish the neckline.

9. Make the sleeves (measure first!) or finish the armholes.

10. Put it all together!

Floating Purls

As so often happens, I discovered this stitch by accident. I was working with the brilliant blue-green Kyoto yarn featured in the Elegant Cardigan (page 31), designing the sweater as I went along. I had decided to start with a slightly dressy, long rib pattern for the bottom of the sweater. This rib was a (K1, P1) pattern on the right side with a purl on the wrong side. As the pattern developed, I realized that the wrong side of this fabric was gorgeous! So, I decided to reverse the pattern for the body of the sweater: a (K1, P1) rib on the wrong side, with a purl stitch on the right side.

At first glance, this looks like a simple garter stitch (where all stitches are knit on both the right and wrong sides). Looking more closely, you'll see that there is more space between the stitches. Alternate stitches appear as purl stitches floating on a smooth background. This really emphasizes the qualities of the yarn, especially yarns with texture and color variations.

On a bulky yarn, this stitch takes on a different look. The spaces between the purls become less and less visible. With a giant yarn, like the Weekend felted merino shown in the Granny Bomber (page 36), all you see are the tightly packed purl stitches. This produces the yarn-flattering look of a garter stitch with the stability of a rib stitch.

This stitch will work with just about any sweater shape; it increases and decreases easily, drapes well, and doesn't cling. The right project will largely be determined by the weight of the yarn you choose. This stitch creates an elegant fabric with a lightweight yarn, a highly textured fabric with a medium-weight yarn, and creates some interest in a super-chunky yarn. The range of yarn weights that work with this stitch are demonstrated with the patterns in this section.

The two raglan sleeve patterns, the Raglan Turtleneck and the Granny Bomber, have very simple shaping and finishing techniques and are knit in big gauges. These are good projects for beginners and will perhaps require two weekends for experienced knitters.

Stitch Patterns Used in This Chapter

Floating Purl
Odd number of sts
Row 1 (RS): KS, purl across, KS.
Row 2 (WS): KS, K1, (P1, K1) across, KS.
Rep rows 1 and 2.

Floating Purl with 1-Stitch Border
Odd number of sts
Row 1 (RS): KS, K1, purl across, K1, KS.
Row 2 (WS): KS, P1, K1, (P1, K1) across, P1, KS.
Rep rows 1 and 2.

Tips

Flip it: The reverse side of this stitch makes a simple choice for a complementary stitch pattern you can use for trim. The "purl back rib"—(K1, P1) on the right side, purl the wrong side—is used in two of the sweaters shown here (and elsewhere in the book). Because it's simply the back side of the same stitch, it will always knit to the same gauge as the Floating Purl stitch.

Edges: With either side on the right side, the Floating Purl stitch works well for exposed fabric edges. Like a rib, it will resist curling and lie flat. Unlike most ribs, it will not cling or pull in. That makes it great for the bottom edge of a long sweater, where a straight line of fabric is more attractive than the traditional pulled-in look of a bottom rib. On a vertical edge, like a button band, the stitch may curl slightly; a light blocking should take care of that.

Seams: Like a garter stitch, the Floating Purl stitch doesn't provide a great edge for seaming. For the patterns here, I add various edge stitches for better seams (in addition to the KS selvage stitch).

Floating Purl with 2-Stitch Rib Border

Odd number of sts
Row 1 (RS): KS, K2, purl across, K2, KS.
Row 2 (WS): KS, P2, K1, (P1, K1) across, P2, KS.
Rep rows 1 and 2.

Floating Purl with 3-Stitch Rib Border

Odd number of sts
Row 1 (RS): KS, K1, P1, K1, purl across, K1, P1, K1, KS.
Row 2 (WS): KS, P3, K1, (P1, K1) across, P3, KS.
Rep rows 1 and 2.

Purl Back Rib (back of Floating Purl)

Odd number of sts
Row 1 (RS): KS, K1, (P1, K1) across, KS.
Row 2 (WS): KS, purl across, KS.
Rep rows 1 and 2.

Rolled Reverse Stockinette Band

Any number of sts
Rows 1, 3, 5 (RS): KS, purl across, KS.
Rows 2, 4, 6 (WS): Knit across.
Row 7 (RS): Knit across.
Row 8 (WS): KS, purl across, KS.
Rows 9–14: Rep rows 3–8.
Rows 15–19: Rep rows 3–7.

Banded Shell

This sweater can be made in gauges of 15–20 stitches = 4" (worsted range).

Model sweater body knit in one strand of Garnstudio Cotton rayon (54% Egyptian cotton,
46% viscose; 50 g, 110 m per skein) with one strand of Trendsetter Yarns Charm (77%
polyester, 23% polyamide tactel; 20 g, 86 m per skein) on #7 needles.

Model gauge: 20 sts and 24 rows = 4" in patt

Model sweater contrast bands knit in two strands of Cotton Viscose (54% cotton,
46% rayon) on #7 needles.

Model trim gauge: 15 sts = 4" in reverse St st

*H*ave fun mixing yarns for this sweater. As shown in the model, it's a great way to use flag yarns; pair them up with a solid yarn and knit with two strands. Alternately, pair a variegated yarn with a complementary solid yarn for the contrast bands.

    The gauge of the contrast bands doesn't need to match, but it should be in the same range.

RIGHT

Sample body knit in two strands of Skacel Riviera Multi
    (45% cotton, 30% linen, 25% rayon; 50 g, 110
    yds per skein) on #8 needles.

Sample gauge: 17 sts and 26 rows = 4" in patt

Sample bands knit in Jaeger Albany (100% mercerized
    cotton; 50 g, 105 m per skein) on #6 needles.

Sample trim gauge: 19 sts = 4" in reverse St st

Yarn Required (in yards)

The yardage indicated is the total yards per strand used. If you're using a single yarn for the body of the sweater and a single, different yarn for the bands, use the figures for MC and CC respectively.

    The model sweater was knit with one strand of novelty yarn (yarn A) together with one strand of smooth yarn (yarn B) for the MC. Two strands of yarn B are used for CC. In this case, for yarn A, use the amount shown in the table for MC. For yarn B, you'll need the total amount for MC plus twice the amount shown for CC.

Finished Sweater Size	33"	36"	40"	44"	48"
Gauge (No. sts = 4")			Yards		
15	625 MC	775 MC	875 MC	975 MC	
	200 CC	225 CC	250 CC	250 CC	
16	575 MC	675 MC	825 MC	925 MC	1,025 MC
	200 CC	225 CC	225 CC	250 CC	275 CC
17	625 MC	725 MC	875 MC	1,000 MC	1,100 MC
	225 CC	225 CC	250 CC	275 CC	300 CC
18	675 MC	775 MC	950 MC	1,075 MC	
	225 CC	250 CC	275 CC	300 CC	
19	700 MC	825 MC	1,000 MC	1,125 MC	
	250 CC	250 CC	275 CC	300 CC	
20	750 MC	875 MC	1,050 MC		
	250 CC	275 CC	300 CC		

Additional Materials

✦   Needles for sweater body, the size used for gauge swatch

✦   Needles for contrast bands, the appropriate size for CC

Before You Begin:

1. Make a gauge swatch in MC in the Floating Purl pattern. This sweater can be made in gauges of 15–20 stitches = 4" (worsted range).

2. Determine the sweater size that you want to make (see page 10).

3. Identify the pattern number that will produce the sweater size that you want (see pages 10–12). Directions are given for pattern number 1; changes for pattern numbers 2, 3, 4, and 5 are in parentheses. Note that a pattern number 1 does not necessarily mean a 33" sweater size!

4. Review the sweater measurements in the table below. The letters in the table correspond to the letters on the diagrams. Adjust lengths as necessary for the fit that you want.

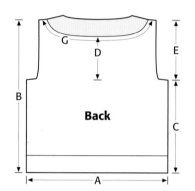

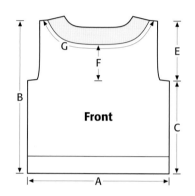

Measurement G is the total inside length
of the neckband, including back and front.
Hip band is knit in place; neckband is added later.

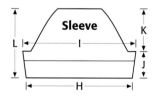

Cuff band is knit in place.

Sweater Measurements (in inches)

Finished Sweater Size	33	36	40	44	48
A. Back width, front width	16½	18	20	22	24
B. Back length, front length (includes hip band and neckband)	19	20½	21½	22	23
C. Length to armhole	10½	11½	12	12	12
D. Length from armhole to back neck	5½	6	6½	7	8
E. Length from armhole to shoulder	7½	8	8½	9	10
F. Length from armhole to front neck	4½	5	5½	6	7
G. Neckband length	25	27	29	31	34
H. Sleeve width at cuff	12½	13½	14½	15½	16½
I. Sleeve width at underarm	13½	14½	15½	16½	17½
J. Sleeve length to underarm	3	3	3	3	3
K. Length of sleeve cap	5	5½	6	6½	6½
L. Total sleeve length	8	8½	9	9½	9½

Back

1. CO for contrast hip band: Make a gauge swatch for contrast bands using CC and appropriate needle size. Calculate the st-per-inch gauge and multiply by measurement A. CO this number of sts plus 2 selvage sts. Work Rolled Reverse Stockinette Band for 19 rows, ending with completed RS row.

2. Change to MC and appropriate needle size. Start with row 2 (WS) of Floating Purl patt. For body of sweater, there should be a total of 67 (75, 83, 91, 99) sts (including 2 selvage sts). If that is different than the number of sts used in hip band, inc or dec as needed in first row to achieve this number. Distribute incs or decs evenly across width of work.

3. At measurement C, beg armhole shaping: BO 5 (5, 5, 7, 7) sts at beg of next 2 rows. In next 3 (3, 3, 5, 5) RS rows, dec 1 st at each side— 51 (59, 67, 67, 75) sts rem.

4. At measurement D, beg back neck shaping: Work across 16 (19, 21, 21, 23) sts, move center 19 (21, 25, 25, 29) sts to holder, join second ball of yarn, finish row. Working both sides at same time, at each neck edge, BO 3 (4, 4, 4, 4) sts once; BO 2 (3, 4, 4, 4) sts once; BO 2 (2, 3, 3, 3) sts once; BO 2 sts once more; dec 1 st next 2; BO rem 5 (6, 6, 6, 8) sts each side.

Front

1. With CC, CO sts as for back contrast hip band. Work as for back, steps 1–3: 51 (59, 67, 67, 75) sts rem.

2. At measurement F, beg front neck shaping: Work across 17 (20, 23, 23, 25) sts, move center 17 (19, 21, 21, 25) sts to holder, join yarn, finish row. Working both sides at same time, at each neck edge, BO 2 (3, 5, 5, 5) sts once; BO 2 (3, 4, 4, 4) sts once; BO 2 sts once more; dec 1 st next 6 RS rows. BO rem 5 (6, 6, 6, 8) sts on each side.

Neckband

1. Put a permanent seam in one shoulder.

2. Multiply contrast band st-per-inch gauge by measurement G. (This number may range from 100 for a small size at a 4-st-per-inch gauge to 200 for a large size at a 6-st-per-inch gauge.) With CC and appropriate needle size, and RS facing, PU approx this number of sts.

3. Next row (WS), knit across. Next row (RS), work Rolled Reverse Stockinette Band, beg with row 3. Dec 4 sts spaced evenly throughout work every RS row. Work through patt row 19 (a RS row), changing location of decs each time. Rep rows 18–19. BO using a tension that will allow neckline to lie flat.

4. Put a permanent seam in second shoulder, including neckband. Reinforce shoulder seams if desired.

Sleeves

1. Multiply contrast band st-per-inch gauge by measurement H. For each sleeve, with CC and appropriate needle size, CO this number of sts. Work Rolled Reverse Stockinette Band for 19 rows, ending with completed RS row. Inc 1 st at each side in rows 7 and 13.

2. Change to MC and appropriate needle size. Start with row 2 (WS) of Floating Purl patt. For sleeve, there should be a total of 57 (61, 65, 69, 75) sts (including 2 selvage sts). If that is different than number of sts used in cuff, inc or dec as needed in first row to achieve this number. Distribute incs or decs evenly across width of work.

3. At measurement J, beg sleeve cap: BO 4 (4, 4, 5, 5) sts at beg of next 2 rows. Dec 1 st at each side of each RS row until sleeve cap measures 4½ (4½, 4½, 5, 5½)". BO 2 sts at beg of each row until sleeve cap reaches measurement K. BO rem sts.

And Finally

1. Sew in sleeves.
2. Sew side seams and sleeve seams.

Raglan Turtleneck

This sweater can be made in gauges of 10–15 stitches = 4" (chunky range).

Model sweater knit in one strand of Mondial Sharm (56% nylon, 3% polyester metalized, 41% acrylic; 50g, 105 m per skein) with one strand of KKK Clip (100% Egyptian cotton; 100 g, 166 m per skein) on #11 needles.

Model gauge: 13 sts and 17 rows = 4"

*T*his pattern is meant for showing off great texture. The model sweater has a dressy look using a sparkly ribbon held with a solid cotton yarn. Alternately, this pattern is great in a warm and cuddly yarn, such as chenille. For a more casual look, try a big cotton ribbon.

RIGHT

Sample knit in Plymouth Yarn Sinsation (80% rayon, 20% wool; 50 g, 38 yds per skein) on #10½ needles.

Sample gauge: 10 sts and 17 rows = 4"

BOTTOM RIGHT

Sample knit in Bouton d'Or Balzane (55% cotton, 45% nylon; 100 g, 105 m per skein) on #11 needles.

Sample gauge: 12 sts and 20 rows = 4"

Yarn Required (in yards)

Finished Sweater Size	33"	36"	40"	44"	48"
Gauge (No. sts = 4")			Yards		
10			800	875	975
11		775	900	975	1,100
12	775	850	1,000	1,100	1,200
13	850	950	1,100	1,200	
14	925	1,150	1,150	1,300	
15	1,000	1,200	1,300		

Additional Materials

Needles, the size used for gauge swatch

Before You Begin:

1. Make a gauge swatch in the Floating Purl pattern. This sweater can be made in gauges of 10–15 stitches = 4" (chunky range).

2. Determine the sweater size that you want to make (see page 10).

3. Identify the pattern number that will produce the sweater size that you want (see pages 10–12). Directions are given for pattern number 1; changes for pattern numbers 2, 3, 4, and 5 are in parentheses. Note that a pattern number 1 does not necessarily mean a 33" sweater size!

4. Review the sweater measurements in the table below. The letters in the table correspond to the letters on the diagrams. Adjust lengths as necessary for the fit that you want.

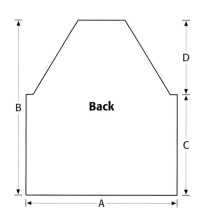
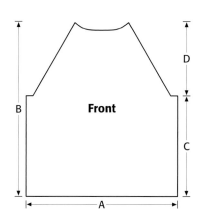
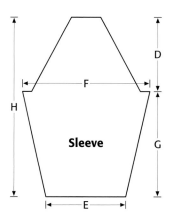

Turtleneck is added later (not shown).

Sweater Measurements (in inches)

Finished Sweater Size	33	36	40	44	48
A. Back width, front width	16½	18	20	22	24
B. Back length, front length* (does not include turtleneck)	19	20	21	21½	22
C. Length to armhole	11	11½	12	12	12
D. Height of raglan armhole shaping	8	8½	9	9½	10
E. Sleeve width at bottom	9	9½	10	11½	13
F. Sleeve width at underarm	14	14½	15	17	19
G. Sleeve length to underarm	10	10	10	10	10
H. Total sleeve length	18	18½	19	19½	20

With a raglan sweater, because the front and back pieces do not extend all the way to the shoulder, the full length of the sweater will be slightly longer than this measurement.

Back

1. CO 51 (55, 59, 67, 73) sts. Work in Floating Purl with 1-Stitch Border patt.

2. At measurement C, beg raglan armhole shaping: BO 2 (2, 2, 3, 3) sts at beg of next 2 rows. Cont Floating Purl with 1-Stitch Border patt, dec 1 st at each side (P2tog just inside border st) 17 (18, 19, 20, 22) times, evenly spaced between armhole and measurement D. Move rem 13 (15, 17, 21, 23) sts to holder.

Front

1 Work as for back until 19 (21, 23, 27, 29) sts rem.

2. Beg front neck shaping: On RS row, KS, K1, P2tog, P4, move center 3 (5, 7, 11, 13) sts to holder, join second ball of yarn, P4, P2tog, K1, KS. Working both sides at same time, on each side, dec 1 st at neck edge and 1 st at shoulder edge next 2 RS rows. Put rem 3 sts on holder.

Sleeves

1. For each sleeve, CO 29 (31, 33, 37, 41) sts. Work in Floating Purl with 1-Stitch Border patt. Inc 1 st at each side (just inside border st) 9 (9, 10, 10, 10) times evenly spaced until sleeve reaches measurement G—47 (49, 53, 57, 61) sts.

2. At measurement G, work raglan armhole shaping as for back. Put rem 9 (9, 11, 11, 11) sts on holder.

Neck Finishing

1. Put a permanent seam in 3 of the 4 raglan shoulder seams, leaving 1 back seam open.

2. For collar, PU 12 (14, 16, 20, 22) sts from back, 9 (9, 11, 11, 11) sts from one sleeve, about 15 (17, 19, 23, 25) sts from front, 9 (9, 11, 11, 11) sts from second sleeve. There should be a total of about 45 (49, 57, 65, 69) sts. (You will need an odd number of sts). Inc 1 st in first row, if necessary, to make an odd number of sts.

3. Work turtleneck with RS of Floating Purl patt on inside of sweater for 7" (or desired length). BO loosely. When collar is folded over, right side of patt will be on outside of sweater.

4. Put a permanent seam in fourth shoulder seam, including collar.

And Finally

Sew side seams and sleeve seams.

Elegant Cardigan

This sweater can be made in gauges of 10–15 stitches = 4" (chunky range).

Model sweater knit in Artfibers Kyoto (69% spun silk, 25% super kid mohair, 6% extra fine wool; 50 g, 110 yds per skein) on #10½ needles.

Model gauge: 13 sts and 17 rows = 4" in patt

This pattern is meant for showing off fine luxury yarns—delicate, lightweight yarns that knit up soft as a cloud. The model sweater is made in a sumptuous silk-and-mohair blend. Try other light and silky fibers with a little loft, such as angora, cashmere, or a lightweight pure silk. Make sure the fabric is light enough to fold the button bands.

RIGHT

Sample knit in Artfibers Chai (100% Tussah silk; 50 g, 165 yds per skein) on #8 needles.

Sample gauge: 15 sts and 26 rows = 4" in patt

Yarn Required (in yards)

Finished Sweater Size	33"	36"	40"	44"	48"
Gauge (No. sts = 4")			Yards		
10			1,075	1,125	1,200
11		1,000	1,200	1,250	1,325
12	975	1,125	1,325	1,400	1,475
13	1,075	1,225	1,450	1,525	
14	1,150	1,500	1,500	1,650	
15	1,250	1,550	1,700		

Additional Materials

✦ Needles, the size used for gauge swatch

✦ Needles one or two sizes smaller

✦ 6 buttons (or desired number)

Before You Begin:

1. Make a gauge swatch in the Floating Purl pattern. This sweater can be made in gauges of 10–15 stitches = 4" (chunky range).

2. Determine the sweater size that you want to make (see page 10).

3. Identify the pattern number that will produce the sweater size that you want (see pages 10–12). Directions are given for pattern number 1; changes for pattern numbers 2, 3, 4, and 5 are in parentheses. Note that a pattern number 1 does not necessarily mean a 33" sweater size!

4. Review the sweater measurements in the table below. The letters in the table correspond to the letters on the diagrams. Adjust lengths as necessary for the fit that you want.

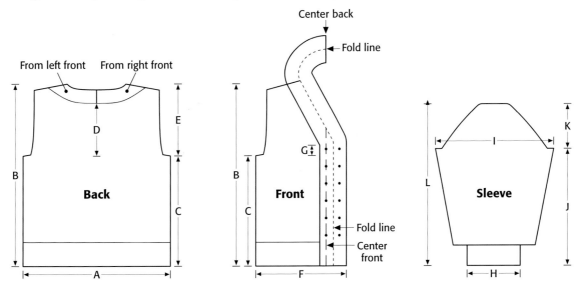

Sweater Measurements (in inches)

Finished Sweater Size	33	36	40	44	48
A. Back width	16½	18	20	22	24
B. Back length, front length (not including neckband)	24½	25	25½	26	26½
C. Length to armhole	16	16	16	16	16
D. Length from armhole to back neck	6	6½	7	7½	8
E. Length from armhole to shoulder	8	8½	9	9½	10
F. Front width (inc double-sided button band)	11½	12	13	14	15
G. Length from armhole to front neck	1½	1½	2	2	2
H. Sleeve width at cuff	7½	7½	8	8½	8½
I. Sleeve width at underarm	14½	15½	16½	18	19
J. Sleeve length to underarm	15½	17	17	17	17
K. Length of sleeve cap	5	5½	6	6½	6½
L. Total sleeve length	20½	22½	23	23½	23½

Back

1. CO 51 (55, 59, 67, 73) sts. Work in Purl Back Rib patt for 3½ (3½, 4, 4, 4)". Switch to Floating Purl with 2-Stitch Rib Border patt.

2. At measurement C, beg armhole shaping: BO 3 (3, 3, 4, 4,) sts at beg of next 2 rows, moving border sts as required. Dec 1 st at each side (inside border) of next 3 (3, 3, 4, 4) RS rows—39 (43, 47, 51, 57) sts rem.

3. At measurement D, beg back neck shaping: Work across 13 (14, 16, 17, 19) sts, join second ball of yarn, BO center 13 (15, 15, 17, 19) sts, finish row. Working both sides at same time, BO 2 sts at each neck edge 2 (3, 3, 4, 4) times.

4. AT SAME TIME, at measurement E, beg shoulder shaping: BO 4 (4, 5, 4, 5) sts at each side. BO rem 5 (4, 5, 5, 6) sts on each shoulder.

Front

1. For each front, CO 38 (40, 42, 46, 48) sts. Work in Purl Back Rib patt for 3½ (3½, 4, 4, 4)".

2. Switch to Floating Purl with 2-Stitch Rib Border patt for 24 (26, 28, 32, 34) sts at outside edge (this includes 1 selvage st on outside edge), PM. For rem 14 sts, cont with Purl Back Rib patt (13 patt sts plus 1 selvage st). These 14 sts will be folded in half to make the button band.

3. At 4" (on RS row) make first buttonhole on right front by knitting 14-st button band as follows: K1, P1, K2tog, YO, K1, P1, K1, P1, K2tog, YO, K1, P1, K1, KS. Rep buttonhole row every 2½" for a total of 6 buttonholes; top buttonhole will be ½" above armhole shaping.

4. AT SAME TIME, at measurement C, work armhole shaping as for back.

5. AT SAME TIME, at measurement G, beg front neck shaping: Beg 2 rows after top buttonhole, dec 1 st just inside button band (on both right and left sides) 9 (12, 12, 15, 15) times over next 15 (16, 16, 17, 18) RS rows. IN FIRST DEC ROW ONLY, work pair of short rows within button band, working center 8 sts only (see "Short Rows," page 135).

6. AT SAME TIME, in last 4 rows of neck shaping, beg shoulder shaping: At side edge BO 4 (4, 5, 4, 5) sts; 2 rows later, BO 4 (3, 4, 4, 5) sts—15 sts rem (13 patt sts of button band plus 2 selvage sts).

7. Cont with both sides of (what is now) the back neckband:

   Rows 1–2: Work pair of short rows on first 4 sts (on outside of neckband).
   Row 3: Work across all sts.
   Rows 4–5: Work pair of short rows on first 4 sts (on inside of neckband).
   Rows 6–8: Work across all sts.

   Rep rows 1–8 until bands are long enough to meet in center back. For best result, baste back piece in place at shoulder and baste neckband to back piece as you knit. BO.

Neck Finishing

1. Sew permanent shoulder seams.

2. Sew back neckband to back neck. Sew neckband ends together at center back.

3. Fold button band/neckband along center st. Align matched pairs of buttonholes and edge with buttonhole st. If desired, work a row of slip-stitch crochet along inside and outside edges of button band/neckband to stabilize fabric (see page 138).

Sleeves

1. For each sleeve, with needles 1 or 2 sizes smaller than main patt, CO 23 (23, 25, 27, 27) sts. Work in Purl Back Rib patt for 3".

2. Switch to Floating Purl with 2-Stitch Rib Border and regular needle size. Inc 8 (8, 10, 12, 12) sts in next row evenly spaced across row—31 (31, 35, 39, 39) sts.

3. From beg of patt st to measurement J, inc 6 (8, 8, 8, 10) times on each side—43 (47, 51, 55, 59) sts. Distribute incs evenly over length of sleeve.

4. At measurement J, beg sleeve cap: BO 4 (4, 4, 5, 5) sts at beg of next 2 rows. Dec 1 st at each side of each RS row until sleeve cap measures 4½ (4½, 4½, 5, 5½)". BO 2 sts at beg of each row until sleeve cap reaches measurement K. BO rem sts.

And Finally

1. Sew in sleeves.

2. Sew side seams, leaving bottom rib open. Sew sleeve seams.

3. Sew on buttons.

Granny Bomber

This sweater can be made in gauges of 8–10 stitches = 4" (super-chunky range).

Model sweater knit in Classic Elite Yarns Weekend (felted 100% merino wool; 200 g, 120 yds per skein) on #15 needles.

Model gauge: 9 sts and 14 rows = 4" in patt

This is a pattern for showing off a super-chunky yarn. The model sweater uses a giant felted merino, knit to a dense, firm fabric. The body of the sweater is made in a vibrant variegated jewel tone; to tone it down visually, the trim is done in the same yarn in solid black. (Thanks to Ann Gevas at Fengari for this suggestion!) For a great, rough texture, try a thick/thin wool. Or, try a big, casual cotton.

Note that the bands are knit in place, not added on. If you're using a different yarn for the contrast bands, make sure it will knit to the same gauge.

RIGHT

Sample knit in Rowan Biggy Print (100% merino wool; 100 g, 30 m per skein) on #13 needles.

Sample gauge: 8 sts and 13 rows = 4" in patt

BOTTOM RIGHT

Sample knit in Sirdar Denimultra (60% acrylic, 25% cotton, 15% wool; 100 g, 82 yds per skein) on #13 needles.

Sample gauge: 9 sts and 15 rows = 4" in patt

Yarn Required (in yards)

Finished Sweater Size	33"	36"	40"	44"	48"
Gauge (No. sts = 4")			Yards		
8		525 MC	575 MC	625 MC	700 MC
		125 CC	125 CC	150 CC	150 CC
9	525 MC	600 MC	675 MC	725 MC	800 MC
	150 CC	150 CC	150 CC	175 CC	175 CC
10	600 MC	675 MC	750 MC	825 MC	
	150 CC	175 CC	175 CC	200 CC	

Additional Materials

✦ Needles, the size used for gauge swatch

✦ Separating zipper, 20 (20, 22, 22, 22)" long

Before You Begin:

1. Make a gauge swatch in MC in the Floating Purl pattern. This sweater can be made in gauges of 8–10 stitches = 4" (super-chunky range).

2. Determine the sweater size that you want to make (see page 10).

3. Identify the pattern number that will produce the sweater size that you want (see pages 10–12). Directions are given for pattern number 1; changes for pattern numbers 2, 3, 4, and 5 are in parentheses. Note that a pattern number 1 does not necessarily mean a 33" sweater size!

4. Review the sweater measurements in the table below. The letters in the table correspond to the letters on the diagrams. Adjust lengths as necessary for the fit that you want.

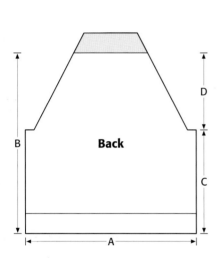

Hip band is knit in place in CC;
neckband is added later.

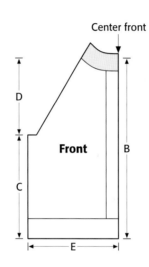

Hip band and center front band
are knit in place in CC;
neckband is added later.

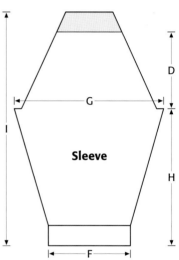

Cuff band is knit in place in CC;
neckband is added on.

Sweater Measurements (in inches)

Finished Sweater Size	33	36	40	44	48
A. Back width	16½	18	20	22	24
B. Back length, front length* (before neckband)	20½	21½	22½	23	23½
C. Length to armhole	12	12½	13	13	13
D. Height of raglan armhole shaping	8½	9	9½	10	10½
E. Front width	8½	9	10	11	12
F. Sleeve width at bottom	9½	9½	10½	10½	11½
G. Sleeve width at underarm	16	17	18	19	20
H. Sleeve length to underarm	15	16	16	16	16
I. Total sleeve length	23½	25	25½	26	26½

*With a raglan sweater, because the front and back pieces do not extend all the way to the shoulder, the full length of the sweater will be several inches longer than this measurement.

Back

1. With CC, CO 37 (41, 45, 49, 55) sts. Work in Purl Back Rib patt for 8 rows. Switch to MC and work in Floating Purl with 3-Stitch Rib Border patt.

2. At measurement C, beg raglan armhole shaping: BO 2 (2, 2, 3, 3) sts at beg of next 2 rows. Cont Floating Purl with 3-Stitch Rib Border patt, dec 1 st at each side (P2tog just inside border sts) 11 (12, 13, 13, 14) times, evenly spaced between armhole and measurement D. Put rem 11 (13, 15, 17, 21) sts on holder.

Front

1. For each front, with CC, CO 21 (23, 25, 27, 29) sts. Work in Purl Back Rib patt for 8 rows. Join MC and work in Floating Purl with 3-St Rib Border patt. Work 4 sts at center edge in CC (3-st border plus selvage st). All other sts are worked in MC. Twist MC and CC yarns on wrong side when changing color.

Tip

To prevent a gap from forming between the band and the body of the sweater, twist the yarns on the wrong side when changing colors. After the last stitch in one color, drop that yarn, and pick up the second yarn from under the first yarn. This will gently lock the first yarn in place. Work the stitches in the new yarn as usual. Twist the yarns this way on both right- and wrong-side rows.

2. At measurement C, work raglan armhole shaping as for back. Cont until there are 2 (2, 3, 3, 3) RS rows rem.

3. Beg front neck shaping (cont side edge decs): BO 4 sts at inside edge (the contrast border). BO 2 sts at inside edge 1 (1, 2, 2, 2) times. Put rem 2 (3, 2, 3, 4) sts on holder.

Sleeves

1. For each sleeve, with CC, CO 21 (21, 23, 23, 25) sts. Work in Purl Back Rib patt for 8 rows. Switch to MC and Floating Purl with 3-Stitch Rib Border patt. Inc 1 st at each side of each sleeve 7 (8, 8, 9, 9) times, evenly spaced until sleeve reaches measurement H—35 (37, 39, 41, 43) sts.

2. At measurement H, work raglan armhole shaping as for back. Put rem 9 sts on holder.

Neckband

1. Sew all 4 raglan shoulder seams with flat seams (see "Flat Seams," page 137).

2. With CC, PU 4 (4, 6, 8, 8) sts from left front before holder, 2 (3, 2, 3, 4) sts from left front holder, 9 sts from left sleeve holder, 11 (13, 15, 17, 21) sts from back holder, 9 sts from right sleeve holder, 2 (3, 2, 3, 4) sts from right front holder, 4 (4, 6, 8, 8) sts from right front—41 (45, 49, 57, 63) sts.

3. Work neckband in Purl Back Rib patt for 6 rows. On each RS row, dec 4 sts evenly spaced around neckband. (To stay in patt, use a K3tog dec at a purl st. Use this dec twice to dec 4 sts.) BO in patt next row.

And Finally

1. Sew side seams and sleeve seams using flat seams.

2. Sew in zipper.

Make No Mistake

I discovered this stitch after buying a simple cotton ribbon. I needed a little red shell to wear with a madras skirt and loved this particular shade. I had never worked with a ribbon yarn and thought it would make for an interesting change. When I got the yarn home, I experimented with different stitch patterns—swatch after swatch of stockinette stitch, cables, lace, you name it. I didn't think any stitch looked good with this particular yarn.

Next time I found myself in Artfibers, I mentioned my problem to Roxanne Seabright. She asked if I had tried a "Mistake Rib." Huh? She explained that a Mistake Rib is a basic (K2, P2) rib done on an odd number of stitches. That way, the columns don't line up and an interesting undulating texture is created. Roxanne was right—it was a terrific marriage of yarn and stitch.

As I experimented more, I found that just about every yarn I have tried looks great in this stitch. It creates a wonderful texture with smooth yarns and is also interesting with textured ones. If knit fairly tightly, it creates an accordion or pleated effect. The springier the yarn, the more dramatic the effect. Knit with a looser tension, with a less elastic yarn, and it becomes almost lacy. If you have a yarn you've been wanting to work with, consider one of these patterns.

Stitch Patterns Used in This Chapter

Mistake Rib
Multiple of 4 + 3
Row 1 (RS): KS, K1, (P2, K2) across, KS.
Row 2 (WS): KS, P1, (K2, P2) across, KS.
Rep rows 1 and 2.

NOTE: *Until you get used to working in this pattern, it's easy to lose your place. As a guide, the fabric created will have vertical columns of knit stitches every four stitches. This column lines up with the second of each pair of knit stitches. This is true on both the right and wrong side of the fabric.*

Seed Stitch
Odd number of sts
All rows: KS, K1, (P1, K1) across, KS.

Broken Twisted Rib
Multiple of 4 + 3
Row 1 (RS): KS, purl all sts across, KS.
Row 2 (WS): KS, P1, (K1, P1) across, KS.
Row 3 (RS): KS, K1tbl, (P1, K1tbl) across, KS.
Row 4 (WS): As row 2.
Row 5 (RS): KS, purl all sts across, KS.
Row 6 (WS): KS, K1, (P1, K1) across, KS.
Row 7 (RS): KS, P1, (K1tbl, P1) across, KS.
Row 8 (WS): As row 6.
Rep rows 1–8.

Tips

Flip it: This stitch is reversible; try it for scarves and wraps.

Trim: Seed stitch makes a great trim stitch. It complements the texture of the rib well. Three of the four featured sweaters use seed stitch for bands. Feel free to try contrasting yarns here. Whether you use a contrasting yarn or your main yarn, expect the gauge to be different than your pattern stitch—you'll need a separate gauge swatch for the trim (please!).

Texture: The way I knit, holding the yarn fairly loosely, this stitch creates a somewhat twisted texture. If you prefer straighter vertical lines, try pulling more tightly on your yarn as you switch from knit to purl and from purl to knit stitches.

Continental style: If you've never tried holding the yarn in your left hand and "picking" the yarn, this is a great time to try. Switching between a knit stitch and a purl stitch is a much smoother motion when the yarn is in your left hand. Rather than using your right hand to move the yarn from back to front (and vice versa), you just use a different angle as you pick up the yarn with your right needle. Thus rib stitches are much faster and easier if you hold the yarn in your left hand. Try it!

Gauge: Fabric knit in this stitch can scrunch up like an accordion. So how do you measure the gauge of such a fabric? At what point of contraction is it relaxed? I try to split the difference between fully stretched out and fully scrunched in. This is how I want it to look when it's worn. So, when it's time to measure the fabric, whether in a gauge swatch or the actual garment, I stretch it out slightly. At this point, the accordion pleats should be visible but not too deep. The resulting fabric still has plenty of room to stretch and will still have a slight cling.

Binding off: If you bind off each stitch in this pattern, the edge of the fabric will flatten out and stretch. While that is okay for edges that need to be very loose (such as the end of a turtleneck collar), it's not great for areas like round necklines or shoulders. To keep the feel of the pattern in these areas, decrease one stitch in each pattern repeat (K2, P2tog) as you bind off.

Simple Shell

This sweater can be made in gauges of 15–20 stitches = 4" (worsted range).

Model sweater knit in Artfibers Cairo (100% cotton ribbon; 50 g, 74 yds per skein) on #8 needles.

Model gauge: 18 sts and 29 rows = 4" in patt

C 20a 150%

*T*his shell will look great in just about any yarn you can imagine. As shown in a flat cotton ribbon, it makes a great everyday summer shell. But use a rayon ribbon, and it will shine. Use a metallic fiber and a little eyelash and it becomes evening wear. With a variegated yarn, try making the bands in a solid, contrasting yarn. Experiment!

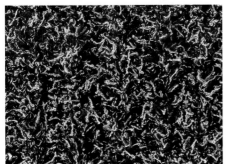

LEFT

Sample knit in Berroco Glacé (100% rayon; 1.75 oz, 75 yds per skein) on #7 needles.
Sample gauge 20 sts and 32 rows = 4" in patt

BOTTOM LEFT

Sample knit in Ironstone Yarns Desert Flower (88% rayon, 7% polyester, 5% metalized thread; 50 g, 112 yds per skein) on #7 needles.
Sample gauge: 17 sts and 26 rows = 4" in patt

Yarn Required (in yards)

Finished Sweater Size	33"	36"	40"	44"	48"
Gauge (No. sts = 4")			Yards		
15		575	675	750	850
16	500	600	725	800	925
17	550	650	775	875	975
18	575	700	800	925	
19	625	725	850	975	
20	650	775	900		

Additional Materials

Needles, the size used for gauge swatch

Before You Begin:

1. Make a gauge swatch in the Mistake Rib pattern. This sweater can be made in gauges of 15–20 stitches = 4" (worsted range).

2. Determine the sweater size that you want to make (see page 10).

3. Identify the pattern number that will produce the sweater size that you want (see pages 10–12). Directions are given for pattern number 1; changes for pattern numbers 2, 3, 4, and 5 are in parentheses. Note that a pattern number 1 does not necessarily mean a 33" sweater size!

4. Review the sweater measurements in the table below. The letters in the table correspond to the letters on the diagrams. Adjust lengths as necessary for the fit that you want.

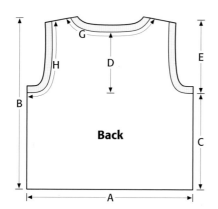 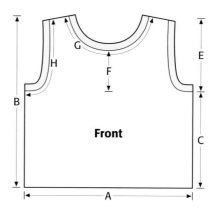

Measurement G is the neckband length, inside edge, back and front;
measurement H is the armband length, inside edge, back and front,
where "inside" means the edge against the garment fabric (the long edge).
Neckband and armbands are added later.

Sweater Measurements (in inches)

Finished Bust Size	33	36	40	44	48
A. Back width, front width	16½	18	20	22	24
B. Back length, front length (does not include neckband)	17½	18	19	19½	20½
C. Length to armhole	10	10	10½	10½	11
D. Length from armhole to back neck	5½	6	6½	6½	7
E. Length from armhole to shoulder	7	7½	8	8½	9
F. Length from armhole to front neck	4	4	4½	4½	5
G. Neckband length	20	22	24	27	29
H. Armband length	18	20	22	24	26

Back

1. CO 67 (75, 83, 91, 99) sts. Work in Mistake Rib patt to measurement C.

2. Beg armhole shaping: BO 3 (3, 5, 5, 6) sts at beg of next 2 rows. BO 2 (2, 3, 3, 4) sts at beg of next 2 rows. Dec 1 st at each side next 3 (3, 4, 4, 6) RS rows—51 (59, 59, 67, 67) sts rem.

3. At measurement D, beg back neck shaping: Work across 15 (18, 18, 20, 20) sts, join second ball of yarn, BO center 21 (23, 23, 27, 27) sts, finish row. Working both sides at same time, at each neck edge, BO 2 sts; 2 rows later, BO 2 sts; dec 1 st next 2 (3, 3, 3, 3) RS rows.

4. AT SAME TIME, at measurement E, beg shoulder shaping: At each shoulder edge, BO 4 (5, 5, 6, 6) sts; 2 rows later, BO rem 5 (6, 6, 7, 7) sts on each shoulder.

Front

1. Work as for back, steps 1–2. At measurement F, beg front neck shaping. Work across 17 (20, 20, 23, 23) sts, join second ball of yarn, BO center 17 (19, 19, 21, 21) sts, finish row. Working both sides at same time, at each neck edge BO 3 sts; 2 rows later, BO 2 sts; 2 rows later, BO 2 sts; dec 1 st next 1 (2, 2, 3, 3) RS rows.

2. AT SAME TIME, at measurement E, work shoulder shaping as for back.

Neckband

1. Put a permanent seam in one shoulder.

2. Make a gauge swatch in seed st and calculate st-per-inch gauge. Multiply by measurement G. This number may range from 70 for a small size with a 4-st-per-inch trim gauge to 180 for a large size with a 6-st-per-inch trim gauge. PU approx this number of sts, ending with an odd number of sts.

3. Work first row of neckband in seed st patt. Next RS row, dec a total of 8 sts evenly across band by working P3tog 4 times. Next RS row, rep decs (vary the locations of the decs). Next RS row (or at desired width), BO with tension that keeps neckline flat. (If you choose to make the band much wider than ¾", rep above dec patt each RS row.)

4. Put a permanent seam in second shoulder, including neckband. Reinforce shoulder seams if desired.

Armbands

1. Multiply seed st st-per-inch gauge by measurement H. This number may range from 65 for a small size with a 4-st-per-inch trim gauge to 160 for a large size with a 6-st-per-inch trim gauge. PU approx this many sts, ending with an odd number.

2. Work 1 row in seed st patt. Next RS row, dec a total of 8 sts evenly across band by working P3tog 4 times. On next RS row, rep decs (vary location of decs). On next RS row (or at desired band width), BO armband with tension that keeps armbands flat and fitted. (If you choose to make band much wider than ¾", rep above decs on each RS row.)

3. Rep for second armband.

And Finally

1. Check tension in neckbands and armbands. Tighten BO row, if necessary, to desired fit.

2. Sew side seams.

Button Vest

This sweater can be knit in gauges of 15–20 stitches = 4" (worsted range).

Model sweater knit in Artfibers Trulli (48% alpaca, 46% merino wool, 6% elastane; 50 g, 88 yds per skein) on #10½ needles.

Model gauge: 17 sts and 28 rows = 4" in patt

Model trim knit in two strands of Zegna Baruffa Lane Borgosesia (100% wool; 100 g, 196 m per skein)

Model trim gauge: 16 sts = 4" in patt

*T*he best of all worlds—by putting a flat frame around the pieces of this vest, this pattern shows off the pleated look of the Mistake Rib stitch without creating a clingy fabric. The solid bands also make it a great way to show off a variegated yarn. The model sweater is shown in a springy alpaca-wool blend. The springier the yarn you use, the deeper the pleats will be; see the incredible depth of this stitch when knit in Superwash Bazic Wool.

RIGHT

Sample knit in Classic Elite Yarns Bazic Wool (100% Superwash wool; 50 g, 65 yds per skein) on #10 needles.
Sample gauge: 19 sts and 24 rows = 4" in patt

Yarn Required (in yards)

Finished Sweater Size	33"	36"	40"	44"	48"
Gauge (No. sts = 4")			Yards		
15		425 MC	500 MC	600 MC	675 MC
		175 CC	200 CC	200 CC	225 CC
16	375 MC	450 MC	550 MC	625 MC	725 MC
	150 CC	200 CC	200 CC	225 CC	225 CC
17	400 MC	475 MC	575 MC	675 MC	775 MC
	175 CC	200 CC	225 CC	225 CC	250 CC
18	450 MC	500 MC	625 MC	725 MC	
	175 CC	225 CC	225 CC	250 CC	
19	475 MC	550 MC	650 MC	775 MC	
	200 CC	225 CC	250 CC	275 CC	
20	500 MC	575 MC	700 MC		
	200 CC	250 CC	275 CC		

Additional Materials

✦ Needles for sweater body, the size used for gauge swatch

✦ Long circular needles, in appropriate size for CC

✦ 6 buttons (or number desired)

Before You Begin:

1. Make a gauge swatch in MC in the Mistake Rib pattern. This sweater can be made in gauges of 15–20 stitches = 4" (worsted range).

2. Determine the sweater size that you want to make (see page 10).

3. Identify the pattern number that will produce the sweater size that you want (see pages 10–12). Directions are given for pattern number 1; changes for pattern numbers 2, 3, 4, and 5 are in parentheses. Note that a pattern number 1 does not necessarily mean a 33" sweater size!

4. Review the sweater measurements in the table below. The letters in the table correspond to the letters on the diagrams. Adjust lengths as necessary for the fit that you want.

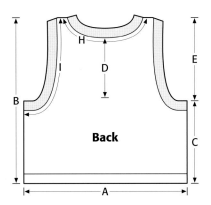

Measurement H is the neckband length, from lower front up to shoulder, around back neck, down to lower front (inside edge). Measurement I is the inside edge of the armband back and front. Hip band is knit in place; neckband and armband are added later.

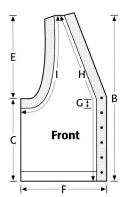

Hip band is knit in place; continuous button band/neckband and armbands are added later.

Sweater Measurements (in inches)

Finished Sweater Size	33	36	40	44	48
A. Back width	16½	18	20	22	24
B. Back length, front length (includes hip band, not neckband)	19	19½	20	20½	21
C. Length to armhole (does not include armband)	9	9	9	9	9
D. Length from armhole to back neck (does not include neckband)	7	7½	8	8	8½
E. Length from armhole to shoulder	10	10½	11	11½	12
F. Front width (does not include button bands)	7½	8½	9½	10½	11½
G. Length from armhole to front neck	1	1	1	1	1
H. Neckband length	50	52	54	56	58
I. Armband length	24	25	27	29	31

Back

1. CO for hip band: With CC and appropriate needle size, make gauge swatch in seed st and calculate st-per-inch gauge. Multiply by measurement A. With CC and appropriate needle size, CO odd number of sts equal to or 1 less than this number. Work in seed st for about 1¼".

2. Change to MC and appropriate needle size; work in Mistake Rib patt. There should be 67 (75, 83, 91, 99) sts. If that is different than the number of sts used in hip band, inc or dec as needed in the first row to achieve this number. Distribute incs or decs evenly across width of work.

3. At measurement C, beg armhole shaping: BO 5 (5, 7, 7, 9) sts at beg of next 2 rows. BO 2 (2, 3, 3, 4) sts at beg of next 2 rows. Dec 1 st at each side of next 3 RS rows. Dec 1 st at each side every other RS row 2 (2, 3, 3, 4) times— 43 (51, 51, 59, 59) sts rem.

4. At measurement D, beg back neck shaping: Work across 12 (14, 14, 16, 16) sts, join second ball of yarn, BO center 19 (23, 23, 27, 27) sts, finish row. Working both sides at same time, dec 1 st at each neck edge next 5 (7, 7, 8, 8) RS rows.

5. AT SAME TIME, at measurement E, BO rem 7 (7, 7, 8, 8) sts on each shoulder.

Front

1. CO for hip band: Multiply seed st st-per-inch gauge by measurement F. For each side, with CC and appropriate needle size, CO odd number of sts equal to or 1 less than this number. Work in seed st for same number of rows as back hip band.

2. Change to MC and appropriate needle size; work in Mistake Rib patt. There should be 31 (35, 39, 43, 47) sts. If that is different than number of sts used in hip band, inc or dec as needed in first row to achieve this number. Distribute incs or decs evenly across width of work.

3. At measurement C, work armhole shaping as for back.

4. AT SAME TIME, at measurement G, beg front neck shaping: Dec 1 st at neck edge a total of 12 (16, 16, 19, 19) times, evenly spaced between measurement G and shoulder.

5. AT SAME TIME, at measurement E, BO rem 7 (7, 7, 8, 8) sts at shoulder.

Neckband

1. Put a permanent seam in both shoulders. Reinforce seams if desired.

2. Multiply seed st st-per-inch gauge by measurement H. This number may range from 200 for a small size at a 4-st-per-inch gauge to 350 for a large size at a 6-st-per-inch gauge. With CC and appropriate (circular) needle size, PU approx this number of sts. Start at bottom front, go up to shoulder, across back neck, and down to bottom front. End with an odd number of sts.

3. Work 1 row in seed st patt. On each side, mark st in front closest to corner of V-neck. Mark 2 matching points in back where neckline is most curved. On all RS rows, inc 2 sts at each front V point (make 1 st on either side of marked st). AT SAME TIME, in every RS row, dec 4 sts in back of neckband near curve points (work P3tog in 2 places). Change location of back neck decs each row. Work neckband for approx ⅝".

4. Mark location for buttonholes on right front: Place top buttonhole at V point. Place lowest buttonhole near bottom, centered within span of hip band. Space additional buttonholes evenly between these 2 buttonholes (see "Buttonholes," page 135). Work buttonholes in next row. Work until 1 less row than hip band.

5. BO neckband. Check often that finished edge lies flat; tighten or loosen tension as needed (or change needle size) to get correct tension.

Armbands

1. Multiply seed st st-per-inch gauge by measurement I. This number may range from 90 for a small size at a 4-st-per-inch gauge to 190 for a large size at a 6-st-per-inch gauge. With CC and appropriate needle size, PU about this number of sts, ending with an odd number of sts.

2. Work armband in seed st. Each RS row, work P3tog twice near lower front and lower back, where band is most curved. Change location of dec in each row. Work until 1 less row than hip bands.

3. BO armband on next row. Check often to make sure finished edge lies flat; tighten or loosen tension as needed (or change needle size) to get correct tension.

4. Rep for second armband.

And Finally

1. Check tension in neck and armbands. Tighten BO row, if necessary, to desired fit.

2. Sew side seams.

3. Sew on buttons.

Twisted-Yoke Pullover

This sweater can be made in gauges of 15–20 stitches = 4" (worsted range).

Model sweater knit in 2 strands of Artfibers Shiva (50% silk, 50% cashmere; 50 g, 133 yds per skein) on #10½ needles.

Model gauge: 16 sts and 22 rows = 4" in patt

*T*his pattern calls for a smooth yarn like Shiva, a luxurious silk-and-cashmere blend. For a similar effect, try other luxury fibers, like the alpaca-and-silk blend called Success. Both of these are DK-weight yarns and are worked with two strands held together. A heavier-weight yarn, such as Goa, held single stranded, also looks great here.

LEFT

Sample knit in 2 strands of Cascade Yarns Success (50% alpaca, 50% silk; 50 g, 123 yds per skein) on #10 needles.

Sample gauge: 16 sts and 25 rows = 4" in patt

BOTTOM LEFT

Sample knit in GGH Goa (50% cotton, 50% acrylic; 50 g, 60 m per skein) on #10 needles.

Sample gauge: 15 sts and 22 rows = 4" in patt

Yarn Required (in yards)

Finished Sweater Size	33"	36"	40"	44"	48"
Gauge (No. sts = 4")			Yards		
15		1,100	1,300	1,400	1,550
16	1,075	1,175	1,375	1,500	1,675
17	1,150	1,275	1,475	1,600	1,775
18	1,225	1,350	1,575	1,725	
19	1,300	1,425	1,675	1,825	
20	1,375	1,500	1,775		

Additional Materials

Needles, the size used for gauge swatch

Before You Begin:

1. Make a gauge swatch in the Mistake Rib pattern. This sweater can be made in gauges of 15–20 stitches = 4" (worsted range).

2. Determine the sweater size that you want to make (see page 10).

3. Identify the pattern number that will produce the sweater size that you want (see pages 10–12). Directions are given for pattern number 1; changes for pattern numbers 2, 3, 4, and 5 are in parentheses. Note that a pattern number 1 does not necessarily mean a 33" sweater size!

4. Review the sweater measurements in the table below. The letters in the table correspond to the letters on the diagrams. Adjust lengths as necessary for the fit that you want.

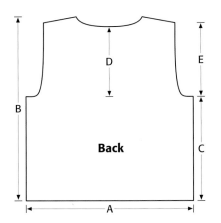
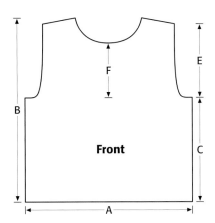
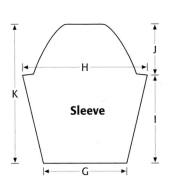

Turtleneck is added later (not shown).

Sweater Measurements (in inches)

Finished Sweater Size	33	36	40	44	48
A. Back width, front width	16½	18	20	22	24
B. Back length, front length	18½	20	21	21½	22½
C. Length to armhole	10½	11½	12	12	12
D. Length from armhole to back neck	7	7½	8	8½	9½
E. Length from armhole to shoulder	7½	8	8½	9	10
F. Length from armhole to front neck	5½	5½	6	6½	7½
G. Sleeve width at bottom	9	9½	10	11½	13
H. Sleeve width at underarm	14	14½	15	17	19
I. Sleeve length to underarm	10	10	10	10	10
J. Length of sleeve cap	5½	5½	6	6½	7
K. Total sleeve length	15½	15½	16	16½	17

Back

1. CO 67 (75, 83, 91, 99) sts. Work in Mistake Rib patt to measurement C.

2. Beg armhole shaping: BO 5 (5, 5, 7, 7) sts at beg of next 2 rows. Dec 1 st at each side next 3 (3, 3, 5, 5) RS rows—51 (59, 67, 67, 75) sts rem.

3. At 1" past armhole, beg with RS row, change to Broken Twisted Rib patt.

4. At measurement D, beg back neck shaping: Work across 15 (19, 20, 20, 22) sts, move center 21 (21, 27, 27, 31) sts to holder, join second ball of yarn, finish row. Working both sides at same time, dec 1 st at each neck edge next 3 RS rows.

5. AT SAME TIME, at measurement E, beg shoulder shaping: At each shoulder edge, BO 6 (8, 8, 8, 9) sts; 2 rows later, BO rem 6 (8, 9, 9, 10) sts.

Front

1. Work as for back, steps 1–3. At measurement F, beg front neck shaping. Work across 20 (24, 26, 26, 28) sts, move center 11 (11, 15, 15, 19) sts to holder, join second ball of yarn, finish row. Working both sides at same time, at each neck edge, BO 2 sts; 2 rows later, BO 2 sts; dec 1 st next 4 (4, 5, 5, 5) RS rows.

2. AT SAME TIME, at measurement E, work shoulder shaping as for back.

Collar

1. Put a permanent seam in one shoulder.

2. With RS facing, PU collar sts as follows (give or take 1 or 2): 5 sts from back side neck, 21 (21, 27, 27, 31) sts from back holder, 5 sts from back side neck, 13 sts from front side neck, 11 (11, 15, 15, 19) sts from front holder, 13 sts from front side neck—68 (68, 78, 78, 86) sts total.

3. Next row (WS), knit across. IN THE NEXT ROW, inc or dec 1 or 2 sts to achieve total number of sts equal to a multiple of 4 plus 3 (for example, 67, 71, 75, 79, 83, 87). Switch to Mistake Rib patt. For a turtleneck, remember that inside of sweater body will fold over and become RS of turtleneck. Work for 5" (or desired length). BO with very loose tension.

4. Put a permanent seam in second shoulder, including collar. Reinforce shoulder seams if desired.

Sleeves

1. For each sleeve, CO 33 (37, 41, 49, 53) sts. To set up patt, knit 1 row on WS. Next (RS) row, switch to Broken Twisted Rib patt, starting with patt row 1 (RS). Inc 1 st on each side in row 6 of cuff patt. Work a total of 13 rows of Broken Twisted Rib patt, ending with patt row 5 (RS).

2. Switch to Mistake Rib patt, starting with patt row 2 (WS). Next RS row, inc 1 st at each side. Inc 1 st at each side 8 more times, evenly spaced between cuff and measurement I—53 (57, 61, 69, 73) sts.

3. At measurement I, beg sleeve cap: BO 4 (4, 4, 5, 5) sts at beg of next 2 rows. Dec 1 st at each side of each RS row until sleeve cap measures 4½ (4½, 4½, 5, 5½)". BO 2 sts at beg of each row until sleeve cap reaches measurement J. BO rem sts.

And Finally

1. Sew in sleeves.

2. Sew side seams and sleeve seams.

Reach for the Stars

*I*found this stitch when I was playing with a luxurious cashmere-blend yarn. It was a beautiful yarn with a smooth, warm texture and a soft, variegated color scheme. The yarn looked great in virtually every stitch pattern I tried, but I was looking for something special, something as elegant as the yarn itself. After trying a number of stitches, I tried the "Star Stitch." What a great marriage between yarn and stitch!

The magic of the Star Stitch is worked on the wrong side. Groups of three stitches are purled together, then looped and purled together again. The result is a "star" made of three long stitches that are joined at the bottom. This gives you a great look at individual strands of yarn.

As I have continued to experiment with this stitch, I have found it flattering to most of the smooth-textured yarns I have tried. In particular, it shows off ribbon yarns beautifully—slender, smooth ribbons; wide, shiny ribbons; and big, woven ones—they are all pretty in this stitch! It also works wonders with variegated yarns. Because it is such a tall stitch, it creates small blocks of color rather than the thin lines of color you would see in most stitches.

This stitch tends to look dressy; it's a natural match with luxury fibers or shimmery textures. Alternately, it can turn a smooth, solid yarn into lace. So, experiment!

Stitch Patterns Used in This Chapter

Star Stitch
Multiple of 4 + 3
Row 1 (RS): Knit across.
Row 2 (WS): KS, P3, (make star, P1) across, make star, P3, KS.
Row 3 (RS): Knit across.
Row 4 (WS): KS, P1, (make star, P1) across, KS.
Rep rows 1–4.

Make star: Insert right needle into 3 sts as if to P3tog. Wrap yarn around right needle and pull right needle out of sts, but do not pull sts off left needle. Wrap yarn around right needle a second time. Insert right needle again into same 3 sts, wrap yarn around right needle a third time and finish the purl st, pulling sts off left needle. Note that 3 sts have been worked off left needle, and 3 sts have been made on right needle.

Star Stitch Starter Rows
Multiple of 3
Row 1 (RS): Knit across.
Row 2 (WS): KS, P1, (make star, picking up 2 sts instead of 3, P1) across, KS.
Note that this row will increase 1 st for each star worked.

Tips

The gauge: Note that when you are estimating the stitch gauge, expect up to 30% more stitches per inch (and fewer rows per inch) in the Star Stitch than that indicated for a stockinette stitch on the yarn packaging. You can also expect to use needles two or three sizes larger than suggested. With this unusual gauge, you will need to plan carefully if you want to mix a Star Stitch with other stitch patterns.

Make it easy on yourself: Executing this stitch involves inserting the right needle purlwise into three stitches at once. You need to do that twice in each star, and there are a few thousand stars in a complete sweater. So, make this action as easy on yourself as possible.

+ I find this stitch easiest to work if I use a relatively pointed knitting needle. My first choice is metal needles when I'm working this stitch. The points of my wooden needles are too rounded.
+ Loosely plied yarn can split easily and drive you crazy. You'll have the same problem if you try to use more than one strand. Try yarns that hold together well, such as tubular yarns, chainettes, or ribbons.
+ It is easiest to execute the P3tog action repeatedly if your needle is small and the yarn is loose. It's also easier if the stitches are already loose on the needle, so work the knit rows loosely as well. If it feels tight, try it with a smaller needle and looser tension.

Binding off: If you bind off every stitch on the right side, you will get a natural scallop edging. If you need a straight edge (such as at shoulder seams), decrease one stitch in every four-stitch pattern repeat as you bind off. (K2tog using the stitch between 2 stars and the first stitch of the next star.)

Casting on: There is a similar issue with the cast-on row. If you cast on the number of stitches that are worked in the pattern, the bottom edge will be too wide. To compensate for this, the patterns that follow have fewer stitches cast on (three per star, rather than four) and special directions for the first pattern row to establish the correct number of stitches.

The swatch: Make a substantial-sized gauge swatch for this pattern. Like a rib stitch, I have found that this stitch has fooled me and has come out 5% or 10% narrower than I expected when I expanded from my gauge swatch to a full-garment fabric width. Unlike a rib, it doesn't stretch with wear to make up for it! So, make a good-size swatch to determine the true gauge.

Purl Back Rib (back of Floating Purl)
Odd number of sts
Row 1 (RS): KS, K1, (P1, K1) across, KS.
Row 2 (WS): KS, purl across, KS.
Rep rows 1 and 2.

Seed Stitch
Odd number of sts
All rows: KS, K1, (P1, K1) across, KS.

K1, P1 Rib
Odd number of sts
Row 1 (RS): KS, K1, (P1, K1) across, KS
Row 2 (WS): KS, P1, (K1, P1) across, KS
Rep rows 1 and 2.

Boatneck Shell

This sweater can be made in gauges of 20–25 stitches = 4" (DK range).

Model sweater knit in two shades of Dale of Norway Kolibri (100% Egyptian cotton; 50 g, 105 m per skein) on #8 needles.

Model gauge: 23 sts and 23 rows = 4" in patt

This sweater was designed to show off the great effect this stitch creates with two colors. It is knit in simple stripes, alternating yarns every two rows. But the effect is far more than that—one of interlocking, diamond-shaped stars. The model sweater is made in two shades of the same yarn. Try mixing a solid with a complementary variegated yarn. Or, stay with one color and mix the fiber.

LEFT

Sample knit in Dale of Norway Kolibri and OnLine Filou (33% cotton, 34% nylon, 33% acrylic; 50 g, 100 m per skein) on #9 needles.

Sample gauge: 22 sts and 22 rows = 4" in patt

BOTTOM LEFT

Sample knit in Jo Sharp Desert Garden (65% cotton, 35% microfiber; 50 g, 55 m per skein) and Trendsetter Yarns Sunshine (75% rayon, 25% nylon; 50 g, 85 m per skein) on #10 needles. To compensate for different weights of these yarns, two rows are knit in worsted-weight cotton and six rows are knit in DK-weight rayon.

Sample gauge: 22 sts and 24 rows = 4" in patt

Yarn Required (in yards)

Finished Sweater Size	33"	36"	40"	44"	48"
Gauge (No. sts = 4")			Yards		
20		450 MC	525 MC	575 MC	650 MC
		325 CC	375 CC	425 CC	475 CC
21	425 MC	475 MC	550 MC	600 MC	675 MC
	300 CC	325 CC	400 CC	450 CC	500 CC
22	425 MC	500 MC	575 MC	650 MC	725 MC
	300 CC	350 CC	425 CC	475 CC	525 CC
23	450 MC	525 MC	600 MC	675 MC	750 MC
	325 CC	375 CC	425 CC	500 CC	550 CC
24	475 MC	550 MC	650 MC	725 MC	
	325 CC	400 CC	450 CC	525 CC	
25	500 MC	575 MC	675 MC	750 MC	
	350 CC	400 CC	475 CC	550 CC	

Additional Materials

✦ Needles for sweater body, the size used for gauge swatch

✦ Needles 2 sizes smaller for Purl Back Rib bands

Before You Begin:

1. Make a gauge swatch in MC and CC in the Star Stitch pattern. This sweater can be made in gauges of 20–25 stitches = 4" (DK range).

2. Determine the sweater size that you want to make (see page 10).

3. Identify the pattern number that will produce the sweater size that you want (see pages 10–12). Directions are given for pattern number 1; changes for pattern numbers 2, 3, 4, and 5 are in parentheses. Note that a pattern number 1 does not necessarily mean a 33" sweater size!

4. Review the sweater measurements in the table below. The letters in the table correspond to the letters on the diagrams. Adjust lengths as necessary for the fit that you want.

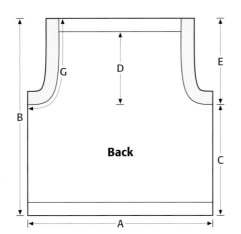
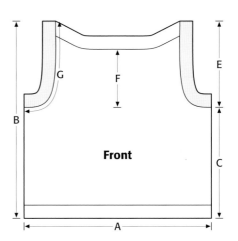

Measurement G is the length of the inside edge of the armband, back and front.
Hip band, back neckband, and front neckband are knit in place; armbands are added later.

Sweater Measurements (in inches)

Finished Sweater Size	33	36	40	44	48
A. Back width, front width	16½	18	20	22	24
B. Back length, front length (includes hip band and neckband)	18	19½	20½	21	21½
C. Length to armhole (does not include armband)	10	11	11½	11½	11½
D. Length from armhole to back neck	6½	7	7½	8	8½
E. Length from armhole to shoulder (includes armband and neckband)	8	8½	9	9½	10
F. Length from armhole to front neck	5	5½	6	6½	7
G. Armband length	20	21½	23	24½	26

Back

1. CO for hip band: With smaller needles, make a gauge swatch with MC in Purl Back Rib patt. Calculate st-per-inch gauge and multiply by measurement A. CO odd number of sts equal to or 1 less than this number. Work in Purl Back Rib for 1½", ending with completed WS row.

2. Change to CC and larger needles and work in Star Stitch patt. In first row, inc as necessary to get 91 (99, 111, 123, 135) sts. Cont in Star Stitch patt, changing yarns every RS row.

3. At measurement C, beg armhole shaping: BO 9 (9, 10, 10, 11) sts at beg of next 2 rows. BO 2 (3, 3, 3, 3) sts at beg of next 2 rows, BO 2 (2, 2, 3, 3) sts at beg of next 2 rows, dec 1 st at each side next 4 (4, 5, 5, 5) RS rows—57 (63, 71, 81, 91) sts rem.

4. Work in patt to measurement D, ending with completed CC (WS) row.

5. Switch to MC and smaller needles. Work in Purl Back Rib patt. In first row, dec 1 st in each star (1 st out of every 4). Dec 1 extra st, if necessary, to get an odd number of sts. Work neckband in Purl Back Rib patt for 1½". BO with firm tension.

Front

1. Work as for back, steps 1–3. At measurement F, beg front neck shaping: Work across 15 (16, 18, 22, 25) sts, move center 27 (31, 35, 37, 41) sts to holder, join second ball of yarn, finish row. Working both sides at same time, at each neck edge, BO 4 (4, 5, 6, 7) sts; 2 rows later, BO 4 (4, 5, 6, 6) sts; 2 rows later, BO 4 (4, 4, 5, 6) sts; 2 rows later, BO rem 3 (4, 4, 5, 6) sts.

2. With MC and smaller needles, PU 15 (16, 18, 22, 25) sts from right side neck, work center 27 (31, 35, 37, 41) sts from holder in Purl Back Rib patt, PU 15 (16, 18, 22, 25) sts from left side neck—57 (63, 71, 81, 91) sts total. Work in Purl Back Rib patt for 1½" (same number of rows as back neckband). BO with firm tension.

Armbands

1. Using a basting yarn, connect front and back at shoulder edges. Note that the armband itself will permanently join the front and back pieces.

2. Multiply st-per-inch gauge for Purl Back Rib patt by measurement G. With MC and smaller needles, PU approx this number of sts, ending with an odd number. Start PU at side edge, cont up piece to shoulder and across to other piece, work down side edge. Work in Purl Back Rib patt. Dec 1 st in first row, if necessary, to get odd number of sts. Each RS row, P3tog at lower curve of armhole on both front and back. Work for 1½". BO with tension that will keep armband flat.

3. Rep for second armband.

And Finally

1. Remove basting yarns from shoulder.

2. Sew side seams, including armbands.

Lace Blouse

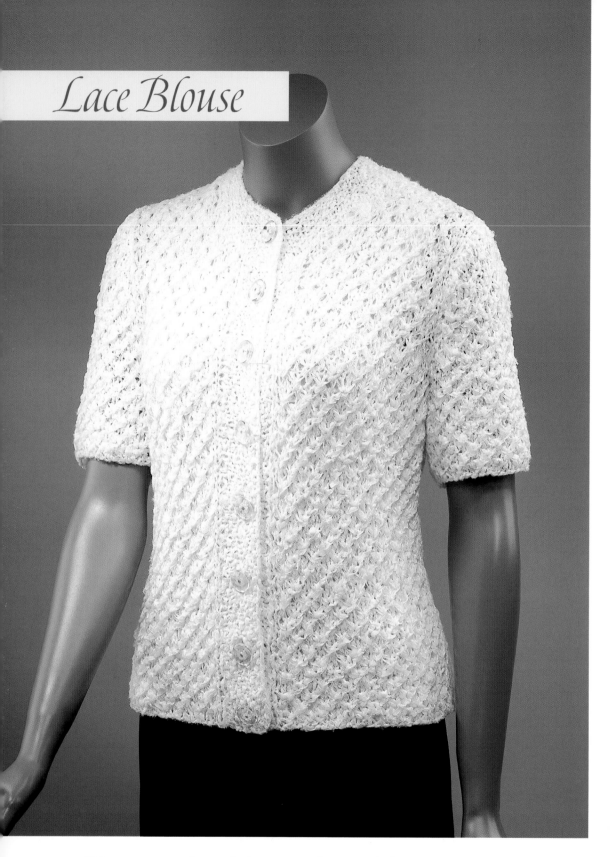

This sweater can be made in gauges of 15–20 stitches = 4" (worsted range).

Model sweater knit in Schachenmayr Diva (60% nylon, 40% new wool; 50 g, 120 m per skein) on #13 needles.

Model gauge: 18 sts and 17 rows = 4" in patt

This sweater was designed with grand ribbons in mind. The long loops of the Star Stitch shows off the full width of a ribbon to great effect. The model sweater is shown in a loosely woven ribbon with a sparkle running through it. Knit with a fairly loose tension, the effect is lacy. Knit to this gauge, a fabric is created that has a natural stretch and slight cling. Smooth ribbons would also be pretty, but for high drama, try a big, bright, variegated ribbon, such as a rayon charmeuse.

RIGHT

Sample knit in Prism Charmeuse Ribbon (100% rayon; 1.75 oz, 68 yds per skein) on #11 needles.

Sample gauge: 16 sts and 16 rows = 4" in patt

Yarn Required (in yards)

Finished Sweater Size	33"	36"	40"	44"	48"
Gauge (No. sts = 4")			Yards		
15		675	775	850	950
16	625	725	850	950	1,025
17	675	775	925	1,025	1,125
18	750	850	1,000	1,100	
19	800	900	1,075	1,175	
20	850	975	1,125		

Additional Materials

✦ Needles, the size used for gauge swatch

✦ Needles 2 or 3 sizes smaller for seed-st trim

✦ 8 (or number desired) buttons

Before You Begin:

1. Make a gauge swatch in the Star Stitch pattern. This sweater can be made in gauges of 15–20 stitches = 4" (worsted range).

2. Determine the sweater size that you want to make (see page 10).

3. Identify the pattern number that will produce the sweater size that you want (see pages 10–12). Directions are given for pattern number 1; changes for pattern numbers 2, 3, 4, and 5 are in parentheses. Note that a pattern number 1 does not necessarily mean a 33" sweater size!

4. Review the sweater measurements in the table below. The letters in the table correspond to the letters on the diagrams. Adjust lengths as necessary for the fit that you want.

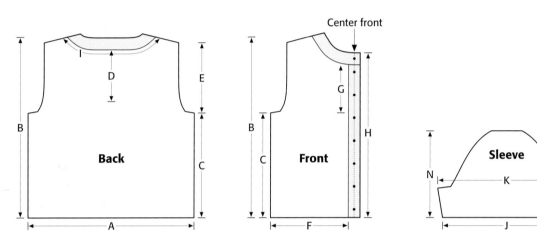

Measurement I is the length of the inside edge of the neckband, from center neck edge to shoulder, across back, to center neck. Neckband and button band are added later.

Sweater Measurements (in inches)

Finished Sweater Size	33	36	40	44	48
A. Back width	16½	18	20	22	24
B. Back length, front length	19	20½	21½	22	23
C. Length to armhole	10½	11½	12	12	12
D. Length from armhole to back neck	7	7½	8	8½	9½
E. Length from armhole to shoulder	7½	8	8½	9	10
F. Front width (not including button band)	7½	8	9	10	11
G. Length from armhole to front neck	5	5½	6	6½	7½
H. Button band length	15½	17	18	18½	19½
I. Neckband length	22	22½	23	24	25
J. Sleeve width at bottom	12	13	14	15	16½
K. Sleeve width at underarm	13	14	15	16	17½
L. Sleeve length to underarm	3	3	3	3	3
M. Length of sleeve cap	5	5½	6	6½	6½
N. Total sleeve length	8	8½	9	9½	9½

Back

1. With larger needles, CO 51 (57, 63, 69, 75) sts. Work 2 rows of Star Stitch Starter Rows—67 (75, 83, 91, 99) sts. Switch to Star Stitch patt and work to measurement C.

2. Beg armhole shaping: BO 5 (5, 7, 7, 7) sts at beg of next 2 rows, dec 1 st at each side next 3 (3, 3, 5, 5) RS rows—51 (59, 63, 67, 75) sts rem.

3. At measurement D, beg back neck shaping: Work across 14 (18, 19, 21, 23) sts, join second ball of yarn, BO center 23 (23, 25, 25, 29) sts, finish row. Working both sides at same time, BO 3 sts at each neck edge.

4. AT SAME TIME, at measurement E, beg shoulder shaping: At each shoulder edge, BO 5 (7, 8, 9, 10) sts; 2 rows later, BO rem 6 (8, 8, 9, 10) sts.

Front

1. For each front, with larger needles, CO 24 (27, 30, 33, 36) sts. Work 2 rows of Star Stitch Starter Rows—31 (35, 39, 43, 47) sts. Switch to Star Stitch patt and work to measurement C.

2. Work armhole shaping as for back—23 (27, 29, 31, 35) sts rem.

3. At measurement G, beg front neck shaping: At neck edge, BO 4 (4, 4, 4, 5) sts; 2 rows later, BO 3 (3, 4, 4, 5) sts; 2 rows later, BO 2 sts; 2 rows later, BO 2 sts; 4 rows later, dec 1 st.

4. AT SAME TIME, at measurement E, work shoulder shaping as for back.

Front Bands and Neckband

1. **Left button band:** With smaller needles, make a gauge swatch in seed st. Calculate st-per-inch gauge and multiply by measurement H. With smaller needles, PU approx this number of sts on left front, ending with an odd number of sts. Work in seed st for 2". BO, using tension to keep band flat.

2. **Right button band:** PU same number of sts as left button band. At 1", work number of buttonholes as desired (see "Buttonholes," page 135). In spacing buttonholes, note that there will be a buttonhole in the top of the 1½"-wide neckband. Work buttonhole 2 sts from right front edge. Cont band to 2". Work button band to same width as left button band. BO.

3. Sew permanent shoulder seams.

4. **Neckband:** Multiply seed st st-per-inch gauge by measurement I. With smaller needles, PU approx this number of sts, ending with an odd number of sts. Work in seed st for 2". P3tog twice every RS row, evenly spaced around neckband. BO with tension to keep neckline flat.

Sleeves

1. For each sleeve, with larger needles, CO 39 (42, 45, 48, 54) sts. Work 2 rows of Star Stitch Starter Rows—51 (55, 59, 63, 71) sts. Switch to Star Stitch patt. At 1" and 2", inc 1 st at each side—55 (59, 63, 67, 75) sts. Work in patt to measurement L.

2. Beg sleeve cap: BO 4 (4, 4, 5, 5) sts at beg of next 2 rows. Dec 1 st at each side of each RS row until sleeve cap measures 1½ (2, 3, 3½, 3½)". BO 2 sts at beg of each row until sleeve cap reaches measurement M. BO rem sts.

And Finally

1. Sew in sleeves.

2. Sew side seams and sleeve seams.

3. Sew on buttons.

Ballet Top

This sweater can be made in gauges of 20–25 stitches = 4" (DK range).

Model sweater knit in Jaeger Albany (100% mercerized cotton; 50 g, 105 m per skein)
   on #10 needles.

Model gauge: 23 sts and 20 rows = 4"

*T*his pattern was designed with a mercerized cotton ribbon in mind. With a slight sheen and a silky texture, this yarn creates a dressy fabric where individual stars are highlighted. The fabric texture is firm, and the sweater shaping is straight, but the crocheted shell edging softens the look. Any smooth yarn will work here, but for a little more sparkle, try a soft, metallic yarn, such as Nobile.

RIGHT

Sample knit in On line Nobile (75% acrylic, 16% cupro, 9% polyester; 50 g, 90 m per skein) on #10½ needles.
Sample gauge: 22 sts and 22 rows = 4"

Yarn Required (in yards)

Finished Sweater Size	33"	36"	40"	44"	48"
Gauge (No. sts = 4")			Yards		
20		1,125	1,275	1,425	1,600
21	1,075	1,200	1,375	1,500	1,700
22	1,100	1,275	1,450	1,600	1,800
23	1,175	1,325	1,525	1,700	1,900
24	1,225	1,400	1,600	1,775	
25	1,300	1,475	1,700	1,875	

Additional Materials

✦   Needles, the size used for gauge swatch

✦   Crochet hook, in size specified for yarn

Before You Begin:

1. Make a gauge swatch in the Star Stitch pattern. This sweater can be made in gauges of 20–25 stitches = 4" (DK range).

2. Determine the sweater size that you want to make (see page 10).

3. Identify the pattern number that will produce the sweater size that you want (see pages 10–12). Directions are given for pattern number 1; changes for pattern numbers 2, 3, 4, and 5 are in parentheses. Note that a pattern number 1 does not necessarily mean a 33" sweater size!

4. Review the sweater measurements in the table below. The letters in the table correspond to the letters on the diagrams. Adjust lengths as necessary for the fit that you want.

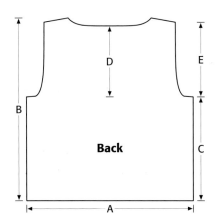
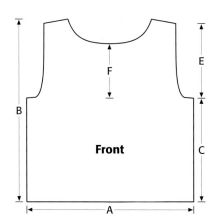
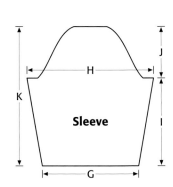

Sweater Measurements (in inches)

Finished Sweater Size	33	36	40	44	48
A. Back width, front width	16½	18	20	22	24
B. Back length, front length	18½	20	21	21½	22½
C. Length to armhole	10½	11½	12	12	12
D. Length from armhole to back neck	7	7½	8	8½	9½
E. Length from armhole to shoulder	7½	8	8½	9	10
F. Length from armhole to front neck	5½	6	6½	7	8
G. Sleeve width at bottom	10	10½	11½	12½	14
H. Sleeve width at underarm	13½	14	15	16	17½
I. Sleeve length to underarm	10	10	10	10	10
J. Length of sleeve cap	5	5½	6	6½	6½
K. Total sleeve length	15	15½	16	16½	16½

Back

1. CO 69 (75, 84, 93, 102) sts. Work 2 rows of Star Stitch Starter Rows—91 (99, 111, 123, 135) sts. Switch to Star Stitch patt and work to measurement C.

2. Beg armhole shaping: BO 5 (5, 6, 7, 7) sts at beg of next 2 rows. Dec 1 st at each side each RS row 5 (5, 6, 7, 7) times—71 (79, 87, 95, 107) sts rem.

3. At measurement D, beg back neck shaping: Work across 19 (21, 22, 24, 28) sts, join second ball of yarn, BO center 33 (37, 43, 47, 51) sts, finish row. Working both sides at same time, at each neck edge, BO 4 (5, 5, 5, 7) sts once; BO 4 (4, 5, 5, 6) sts once.

4. AT SAME TIME, at measurement E, beg shoulder shaping: At each shoulder edge, BO 5 (6, 6, 7, 7) sts once; BO rem 6 (6, 6, 7, 8) sts once.

Front

1. Work as for back, steps 1–2. At measurement F, beg front neck shaping: Work across 23 (25, 28, 31, 35) sts, join second ball of yarn, BO center 25 (29, 31, 33, 37) sts, join yarn, finish row. Working both sides at same time, at each neck edge, BO 2 (3, 4, 5, 6) sts once; BO 2 (2, 4, 4, 6) sts once; *BO 2 sts, rep from * 2 more times; dec 1 st at each neck edge on next 2 RS rows.

2. AT SAME TIME, at measurement E, work shoulder shaping as for back.

Neckband

1. Sew permanent shoulder seams.

2. Crochet shell edge around neck, starting and ending at center back (see "Crocheted Edges," page 140).

Sleeves

1. For each sleeve, CO 42 (45, 48, 51, 57) sts. Work 2 rows of Star Stitch Starter Rows—55 (59, 63, 67, 75) sts. Switch to Star Stitch patt. Inc 1 st at each side 10 times, evenly spaced between bottom of sleeve and measurement I—75 (79, 83, 87, 95) sts.

2. At measurement I, beg sleeve cap: BO 4 (4, 4, 5, 5) sts at beg of next 2 rows. Dec 1 st at each side of each RS row until sleeve cap measures 1½ (2, 3, 3½, 3½)". BO 2 sts at beg of each row until sleeve cap reaches measurement J. BO rem sts.

And Finally

1. Sew side seams and sleeve seams.

2. Crochet shell edge around bottom of sweater and bottom of sleeves.

Shell-Edged Cardigan

This sweater can be made in gauges of 20–25 stitches = 4" (DK range).

Model sweater knit in Artfibers Eden (60% rayon, 30% cashmere, 10% nylon; 50 g, 78 yds per skein) on #10 needles.

Model gauge: 23 sts and 24 rows = 4" in patt

This pattern was designed with luxury yarns in mind. The model sweater is made in a softly variegated rayon and cashmere blend knit into a firm fabric, creating a dressy jacket. Go more casual with a solid-color wool and cashmere blend or a warm cotton ribbon.

LEFT

Sample knit in Debbie Bliss Cashmerino Aran (55% merino wool, 33% microfiber, 12% cashmere; 50 g, 90 m per skein) on #10 needles.

Sample gauge: 23 sts and 21 rows = 4" in patt

BOTTOM LEFT

Sample knit in Colinette Wigwam (100% cotton tape; 100 g, 170 m per skein) on #10 needles.

Sample gauge: 21 sts and 21 rows = 4" in patt

Yarn Required (in yards)

Finished Sweater Size	33"	36"	40"	44"	48"
Gauge (No. sts = 4")			Yards		
20		1,300	1,475	1,625	1,775
21	1,250	1,400	1,575	1,725	1,900
22	1,275	1,475	1,650	1,825	2,000
23	1,325	1,550	1,750	1,925	2,125
24	1,400	1,650	1,850	2,050	
25	1,475	1,725	1,925	2,150	

Additional Materials

- ✦ Needles, the size used for gauge swatch
- ✦ Needles 2 to 3 sizes smaller for rib trim
- ✦ Crochet hook, the size specified for yarn

Before You Begin:

1. Make a gauge swatch in the Star Stitch pattern. This sweater can be made in gauges of 20–25 stitches = 4" (DK range).

2. Determine the sweater size that you want to make (see page 10).

3. Identify the pattern number that will produce the sweater size that you want (see pages 10–12). Directions are given for pattern number 1; changes for pattern numbers 2, 3, 4, and 5 are in parentheses. Note that a pattern number 1 does not necessarily mean a 33" sweater size!

4. Review the sweater measurements in the table below. The letters in the table correspond to the letters on the diagrams. Adjust lengths as necessary for the fit that you want.

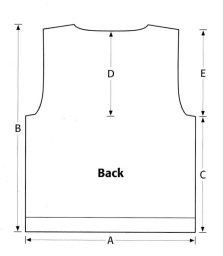 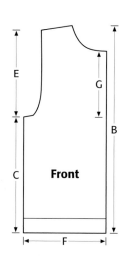 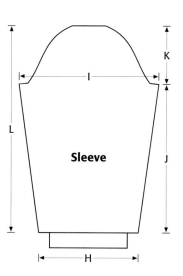

Sweater Measurements (in inches)

Finished Sweater Size	33	36	40	44	48
A. Back width	16½	18	20	22	24
B. Back length, front length	20	21½	23	23½	24½
C. Length to armhole	11	12	13	13	13
D. Length from armhole to back neck	7½	8	8½	9	10
E. Length from armhole to shoulder	8	8½	9	9½	10½
F. Front width	8	8½	9½	10½	11½
G. Length from armhole to front neck	5	5½	6	6½	7½
H. Sleeve width above cuff	9	9½	10	11	11
I. Sleeve width at underarm	14	15	16	17	18
J. Sleeve length to underarm	15½	17	17	17	17
K. Length of sleeve cap	5	5½	6	6½	6½
L. Total sleeve length	20½	22½	23	23½	23½

Back

1. With smaller needles, CO 83 (89, 101, 111, 123) sts. Work 1½" of K1, P1 Rib patt, ending with completed WS row. Inc 8 (10, 10, 12, 12) sts evenly spaced in last row of rib—91 (99, 111, 123, 135) sts. Switch to larger needles and work Star Stitch patt to measurement C.

2. Beg armhole shaping: BO 4 (4, 6, 8, 8) sts at beg of next 2 rows. Dec 1 st at each side each RS row 4 (4, 6, 8, 8) times—75 (83, 87, 91, 103) sts rem.

3. At measurement D, beg back neck shaping: Work across 25 (28, 29, 30, 35) sts, join second ball of yarn, BO center 25 (27, 29, 31, 33) sts, finish row. Working both sides at same time, at each neck edge, BO 4 (4, 5, 5, 6) sts; 2 rows later, BO 4 (4, 4, 4, 5) sts.

4. AT SAME TIME, at measurement E, beg shoulder shaping: At each shoulder edge, BO 6 (7, 7, 7, 8) sts; 2 rows later, BO 6 (7, 7, 7, 8) sts; 2 rows later, BO rem 5 (6, 6, 7, 8) sts.

Front

1. For each front, with smaller needles, CO 39 (42, 46, 53, 57) sts. Work in K1, P1 Rib patt for 1½", ending with completed WS row. Inc 4 (5, 5, 6, 6) sts evenly spaced in last row of rib—43 (47, 51, 59, 63) sts. Switch to larger needles and work Star Stitch patt to measurement C. Work armhole shaping as for back.

2. AT SAME TIME, at measurement G, beg front neck shaping: At neck edge, BO 8 (8, 8, 9, 10) sts; 2 rows later, BO 3 (3, 3, 4, 4) sts; 2 rows later, BO 2 (3, 3, 4, 4) sts; 2 rows later, BO 2 sts; dec 1 st next 3 RS rows.

3. AT SAME TIME, at measurement E, work shoulder shaping as for back.

Neckband

1. Sew permanent shoulder seams.

2. Crochet shell edge, starting at lower front, continuing up and around neck, and back down to lower front (see "Crocheted Edges," page 140).

Sleeves

1. For each sleeve, with smaller needles, CO 41 (41, 45, 49, 49) sts. Work in K1, P1 Rib patt, for 1½", ending with completed WS row. Inc 10 sts evenly spaced in last row of rib—51 (51, 55, 59, 59) sts.

2. Switch to larger needles and work Star Stitch patt, inc 1 st at each side 13 (16, 16, 17, 20) times, evenly spaced between beg of patt st to measurement J—77 (83, 87, 93, 99) sts.

3. Beg sleeve cap: BO 4 (4, 6, 8, 8) sts at beg of next 2 rows. Dec 1 st at each side of each RS row until sleeve cap measures 1½ (2, 3, 3½, 3½)". BO 2 sts at beg of each row until sleeve cap reaches measurement K. BO rem sts.

And Finally

1. Sew in sleeves.

2. Sew side seams and sleeve seams.

A Rib with a Twist

I love this rib. It is simple to knit—(K1, P1) on the right side and (K3, P3) on the wrong side. I often use it on the simplest scarf or shell in place of a stockinette stitch to get a little texture into the fabric. Compared to other ribs (such as the Mistake Rib, page 40), it has much less cling. It seems to add the right amount of shape to any length garment, short or long. It can look very elegant, even on casual yarns.

This stitch is lovely when used on its own. It will not overpower a busy yarn and creates a long, slimming look. But on solid yarns, especially light-colored ones, I'm always tempted to throw in some twists. Three of the sweater patterns in this chapter show off some great cable patterns that blend beautifully with this rib stitch. Because the rib stitch is based on groups of three stitches, all the complementary cable patterns here are also three-way cables. In a three-way cable, two stitches (or groups of stitches) are transferred to a cable needle. The next stitch (or group of stitches) is knit; then the second stitch (or group) is transferred back to the left needle and knit. Finally, the first stitch (or group) is knit from the cable needle. This three-way twist will naturally provide a rounder look than a two-way cable twist; it works well with the "pearl" patterns featured here.

Virtually every yarn I've tried looks great in this stitch. It's a wonderful marriage with textured cottons. It puts easy texture into a complex novelty yarn. But that's just the beginning. Try making your own novelty yarn by holding two or three different strands together. Try luxury fibers. Try thick/thin yarns. Try anything!

Stitch Patterns Used in This Chapter

Triple Rib

Multiple of 6 + 5 (multiple of 12 + 5 when center rib is needed as in Pearl-Twist Shell)

Row 1 (RS): KS, K1, (P1, K1) across, KS.
Row 2 (WS): KS, P3, (K3, P3) across, KS.
Rep rows 1 and 2.

Triple Rib

6-st repeat

KS Knit selvage
● P on RS, K on WS
□ K on RS, P on WS

Tips

Flip it: This stitch (without cables) is reversible; it makes great scarves and shawls.

Self trim: The Triple Rib stitch is "self-trimming," which means it forms clean, uncurled edges. Bottom edges will naturally lie flat; vertical edges may take a little blocking. It works well on long patterns where you don't want a clinging rib to pull in on the bottom.

Plan ahead for cables: Your stitch gauge will change significantly if you start cabling; plan on perhaps 20% more stitches per inch than the same yarn without cables. Also, if you plan to cable, try needles one or two sizes larger to maintain a nice drape to the knitted fabric.

Continental style: As noted with the Mistake Rib, this type of rib pattern is much easier to knit if you hold the yarn with your left hand and "pick." If you've never tried it, try it now!

Triple Rib with Border
Multiple of 6 + 1
Row 1 (RS): KS, K1, (P1, K1) across, KS
Row 2: KS, P1, K3, (P3, K3) across, P1, KS.
Rep rows 1 and 2.

Triple Rib with Border

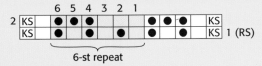

6-st repeat

KS Knit selvage
● P on RS, K on WS
□ K on RS, P on WS

Pearl Twist Yoke Pattern
See charts on page 79.

Cabled Chain Pattern
See chart on page 83.

Cabled Chain Pattern with 4-Stitch Border
See chart on page 83.

Beaded Collar Pattern
See chart on page 83.

Beaded Cuff Pattern
See chart on page 83.

Soft Twist Pattern
See chart on page 93.

Cable Cuff Pattern
See chart on page 93

Pearl-Twist Shell

This sweater can be made in gauges of 20–25 stitches = 4" (DK range).

Model sweater knit with two strands of Artfibers Nazca (100% cotton; 50 g, 165 yds per skein) on #6 needles.

Model gauge: 21 sts and 28 rows = 4" without cables

*I*n this elegant sleeveless shell, a V-shaped yoke begins with a twist of the center rib. The model sweater is shown double-stranded in a thin cotton yarn with an interesting texture: a squiggle shape like fusilli pasta. It has just enough texture to emphasize the depth of the stitch, but not enough texture to hide the detail. Any smooth solid fiber will work here, but for fun, try a yarn with a little (but not too much!) texture. A chainettte yarn is a great choice. Or try a silky ribbon.

LEFT

Sample knit in GGH Capri (48% cotton, 47% modal, 5% nylon; 50 g, 90 m per skein) on #7 needles.

Sample gauge: 24 sts and 32 rows = 4" without cables

BOTTOM LEFT

Sample knit in Artfibers Tiara (75% silk, 25% superkid mohair; 50 g, 148 yds per skein) on #8 needles.

Sample gauge: 20 sts and 26 rows = 4" without cables

Yarn Required (in yards)

Finished Sweater Size	33"	36"	40"	44"	48"
Gauge (No. sts = 4")			Yards		
20		725	850	975	1,075
21	650	750	900	1,025	1,150
22	675	800	950	1,075	1,200
23	725	850	1,000	1,125	1,275
24	750	875	1,050	1,175	
25	775	925	1,100	1,250	

Additional Materials

◆   Needles, the size used for gauge swatch

◆   Cable needle

◆   Crochet hook, the size specified for yarn

Before You Begin:

1. Make a gauge swatch in the Triple Rib pattern. This sweater can be made in gauges of 20–25 stitches = 4" (DK range).

2. Determine the sweater size that you want to make (see page 10).

3. Identify the pattern number that will produce the sweater size that you wan (see pages 10–12). Directions are given for pattern number 1; changes for pattern numbers 2, 3, 4, and 5 are in parentheses. Note that a pattern number 1 does not necessarily mean a 33" sweater size!

4. Review the sweater measurements in the table below. The letters in the table correspond to the letters on the diagrams. Adjust lengths as necessary for the fit that you want.

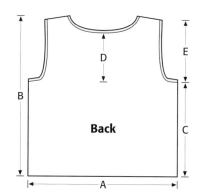 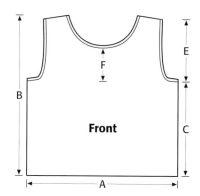

Narrow crocheted edges are added later.

Sweater Measurements (in inches)

Finished Sweater Size	33	36	40	44	48
A. Back width, front width	16½	18	20	22	24
B. Back length, front length	17	18½	19½	20	20½
C. Length to armhole	10	11	11½	11½	11½
D. Length from armhole to back neck	5	5½	6	6½	7
E. Length from armhole to shoulder	6½	7	7½	8	8½
F. Length from armhole to front neck	3	3½	4	4½	5

Back

1. CO 89 (101, 113, 125, 137) sts. Work in Triple Rib patt to measurement C.

2. Beg armhole shaping: BO 3 (6, 6, 6, 6) sts at beg of next 2 rows. Dec 1 st at each side next 3 (6, 6, 6, 6) RS rows—77 (77, 89, 101, 113) sts rem.

3. At measurement D, beg back neck shaping: Work across 29 (29, 33, 37, 41) sts, join sec- ond ball of yarn, BO center 19 (19, 23, 27, 31) sts, finish row. Working both sides at same time, at each neck edge, BO 5 (5, 6, 8, 9) sts; 2 rows later, BO 4 (4, 4, 6, 6) sts; 2 rows later, BO 4 sts; dec 1 st next RS row.

4. AT SAME TIME, at measurement E, beg shoulder shaping: At each shoulder edge, BO 5 (5, 6, 6, 7) sts; 2 rows later, BO 5 (5, 6, 6, 7) sts; 2 rows later, BO rem 5 (5, 6, 6, 7) sts.

Front

1. Work as for back to about 8", ending with completed WS row. Work 37 (37, 43, 49, 55) sts in Triple Rib patt as established, PM. Work next 3 sts, foll row 1 of Pearl Twist Yoke Chart A, PM. Work rem 37 (37, 43, 49, 55) sts in Triple Rib patt as established. On each RS row, move markers 2 sts away from center. Foll Chart A for sts between markers. Cont Triple Rib patt as established in sts outside of markers. As yoke gets wider, rep rows 11–16, working additional sts in patt. When yoke reaches side edges, work Chart B. Rep rows 1–6 of Chart B as needed to shoulders.

2. AT SAME TIME, at measurement C, work armhole shaping as for back.

3. At measurement F, beg front neck shaping: Work across 31 (31, 36, 40, 45) sts, join second ball of yarn, BO center 15 (15, 17, 21, 23) sts, join yarn, finish row. Working both sides at same time, at each neck edge, BO 3 (3, 4, 5, 5) sts; 2 rows later, BO 3 (3, 3, 4, 5) sts; 2 rows later, BO 2 (2, 3, 4, 4) sts; 2 rows later, BO 2 (2, 2, 3, 4) sts; 2 rows later, BO 2 sts; dec 1 st next 4 RS rows.

4. AT SAME TIME, at measurement E, work shoulder shaping as for back.

Neckband

1. Sew permanent seams in both shoulders.

2. Work a single crochet edge around neck, beginning and ending at center back (see "Crocheted Edges," page 140).

Armbands

1. Sew permanent side seams.

2. Work a single crochet edge around both armholes, beg and ending at side seam.

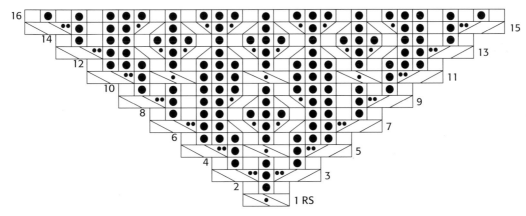

Pearl Twist Yoke Chart A

Rep rows 10-16 until yoke reaches side edges, working additional sts in patt as yoke gets wider, and ending with completed row 16, then beg Chart B.

Pearl Twist Yoke Chart B

6 st repeat

KS Knit selvage

☐ K on RS, P on WS

● P on RS, K on WS

Sl 1 st to cn and hold at back, K1, then P1 from cn

Sl 1 st to cn and hold at front, P1, then K1 from cn

Sl 2 sts to cn and hold at back, K1 from left needle, P sts from cn.

Sl 1 st to cn and hold at front, P2 from left needle, K st from cn.

Sl 2 sts to cn and hold at front, K1, sl last st from cn back to left needle and P this st, then K1 from cn

Cabled Polo

This sweater can be made in gauges of 15–20 stitches = 4" (worsted range).

Model sweater knit with two strands of Artfibers Andes (100% cotton; 50 g, 160 yds per skein) on #9 needles.

Model gauge: 19 sts and 21 rows = 4" in cabled chain pattern

*W*ith more texture than your average cable, this pattern calls for a smooth, light-colored yarn. Alternating long and short cable twists run through the sweater, creating a long, lean look. You may want to try it in a longer length, maybe with a side vent. Tight strings of cabled beads accent the collar and cuffs. As shown—in a soft, brushed cotton—it has a warm, casual feel. Dress it up with the subtle shine of a mercerized cotton or take it into winter with a warm luxury fiber.

RIGHT

Sample knit in Classic Elite Yarns Newport (100% mercerized pima cotton; 50 g, 70 yds per skein) on #10 needles.
Sample gauge: 20 sts and 22 rows = 4" in Cabled Chain pattern

Yarn Required (in yards)

Finished Sweater Size	33"	36"	40"	44"	48"
Gauge (No. sts = 4")			Yards		
15		1,025	1,150	1,250	1,400
16	950	1,100	1,250	1,350	1,500
17	1,000	1,200	1,350	1,450	1,625
18	1,075	1,275	1,425	1,550	
19	1,150	1,375	1,525	1,650	
20	1,225	1,450	1,625		

Additional Materials

✦ Needles, size used for gauge swatch plus next 3 larger-sized needles for collar
✦ Cable needle

Before You Begin:

1. Make a gauge swatch in the Cabled Chain pattern. This sweater can be made in gauges of 15–20 stitches = 4" (worsted range).

2. Determine the sweater size that you want to make (see page 10).

3. Identify the pattern number that will produce the sweater size that you want (see pages 10–12). Directions are given for pattern number 1; changes for pattern numbers 2, 3, 4, and 5 are in parentheses. Note that a pattern number 1 does not necessarily mean a 33" sweater size!

4. Review the sweater measurements in the table below. The letters in the table correspond to the letters on the diagrams. Adjust lengths as necessary for the fit that you want.

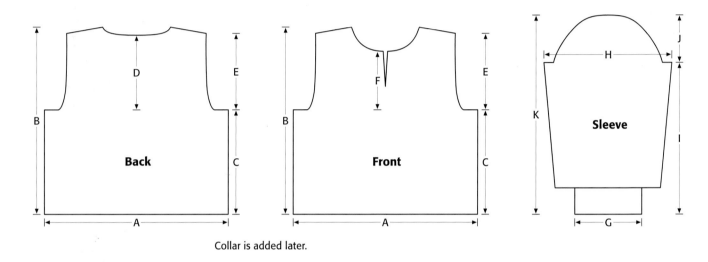

Collar is added later.

Sweater Measurements (in inches)

Finished Sweater Size	33	36	40	44	48
A. Back width, front width	16½	18	20	22	24
B. Back length, front length	19½	20½	21½	22	23
C. Length to armhole	11	11½	12	12	12
D. Length from armhole to back neck	7	7½	8	8½	9½
E. Length from armhole to shoulder	7½	8	8½	9	10
F. Length from armhole to front neck	5	5½	6	6½	7½
G. Sleeve width at cuff	7	7	8	8	9
H. Sleeve width at underarm	14	15	16	17	19
I. Sleeve length to underarm	15½	16½	17	17	17
J. Length of sleeve cap	4½	5	5½	5½	6
K. Total sleeve length	20	21½	22½	22½	23

Cabled Chain Pattern with 4-Stitch Border

12 11 10 9 8 7 6 5 4 3 2 1

12-st repeat

Beaded Cuff Pattern

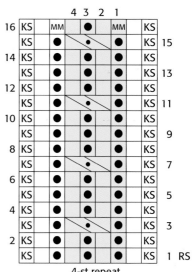

4 3 2 1

4-st repeat

Cabled Chain Pattern

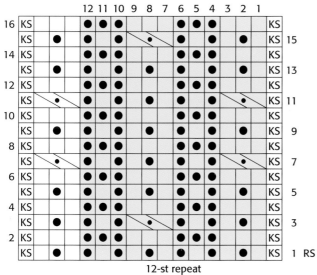

12 11 10 9 8 7 6 5 4 3 2 1

12-st repeat

Beaded Collar Pattern

6 5 4 3 2 1

6-st repeat

KS	Knit selvage
	K on RS, P on WS
●	P on RS, K on WS
MM	M1, K1, M1
⟋	Sl 2 sts to cn and hold at front, K1, sl last st from cn back to left needle and P this st, then K1 from cn

Back

1. CO 65 (77, 85, 89, 97) sts. For sizes 1, 2, and 4, work in Cabled Chain patt, foll chart page 83. For sizes 3 and 5, work in Cabled Chain with 4-Stitch Border patt (see page 83).

2. At measurement C, beg armhole shaping: BO 4 (4, 6, 4, 6) sts at beg of next 2 rows. Dec 1 st at each side next 4 (4, 6, 4, 6) RS rows—49 (61, 61, 73, 73) sts rem.

3. At measurement D, beg back neck shaping: Work across 14 (18, 18, 23, 23) sts, join second ball of yarn, BO center 21 (25, 25, 27, 27) sts, finish row. Working both sides at same time, BO 2 (2, 2, 3, 3) sts at each neck edge.

4. AT SAME TIME, at measurement E, beg shoulder shaping: At each shoulder edge, BO 6 (8, 8, 10, 10) sts; 2 rows later, BO rem 6 (8, 8, 10, 10) sts.

Front

1. Work as for back to measurement C. Work armhole shaping as for back.

2. AT SAME TIME, at measurement C, beg to twist center cable every other RS row. Work to approx 2 (3, 3, 4, 4)" above armhole, ending with completed RS row in which center cable was twisted. Next WS row, inc 1 st at center. Next RS row, work to center cable (which now has 4 sts). Work 2 sts as (K1, KS). Join second ball of yarn. With new yarn, work rem 2 sts of center cable as (KS, K1). Cont in patt, working 2 front sides separately. Each side has a (K1, KS) edge at neck—25 (31, 31, 37, 37) sts on each side.

3. At measurement F, cont front neck shaping: At each neck edge, BO 6 (7, 7, 8, 8) sts; 2 rows later, BO 2 (3, 3, 4, 4) sts; 2 rows later, BO 2 sts; 2 rows later, BO 2 sts; dec 1 st.

4. AT SAME TIME, at measurement E, work shoulder shaping as for back.

Collar

1. Sew permanent shoulder seams.

2. Using same size needles as body of sweater, PU for collar. PU approx 20 (21, 21, 23, 24) sts from front side, 39 (43, 43, 45, 49) sts from back, 20 (21, 21, 23, 24) sts from other front side—79 (85, 85, 91, 97) sts. If total is not equal to a multiple of 6 plus 1, inc or dec in first row to achieve this number. Remember that inside of sweater is RS of collar. Work in Beaded Collar patt (see page 83), foll chart, moving up one needle size every 4 rows. BO in row 17, with tension that will allow collar to fan out to its full width but still lie flat.

Sleeves

1. For each sleeve, CO 29 (29, 33, 33, 37) sts. Work Beaded Cuff patt (see page 83), foll chart for 16 rows. As shown in chart, there are 14 (14, 16, 16, 18) sts increased in last row of patt—43 (43, 49, 49, 55) sts.

2. Work in Cabled Chain with 4-Stitch Border patt. (Note that sizes 1, 2, and 5 will have 2 sts after last full patt rep. Work these sts as K1, KS.) Inc 1 st at each side 8 (10, 10, 11, 13) times evenly spaced between cuff and measurement I—59 (63, 69, 71, 81) sts.

3. At measurement I, beg sleeve cap: BO 4 (4, 5, 5, 6) sts at beg of next 2 rows. Dec 1 st at each side of each RS row until sleeve cap measures 2 (2½, 3, 3, 3)". BO 2 sts at beg of each row until sleeve cap reaches measurement J. BO rem sts.

And Finally

1. Sew in sleeves.

2. Sew side seams (with vent if desired) and sleeve seams.

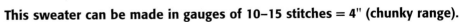

This sweater can be made in gauges of 10–15 stitches = 4" (chunky range).

Model sweater knit in Trendsetter Yarns Dune (41% mohair, 30% acrylic, 12% rayon, 11% nylon, 6% metal; 50 g, 90 yds per skein) on #11 needles.

Model gauge: 11 sts and 14 rows = 4" in patt

This cardigan is easy in several senses of the word. First, it's a snap to make. It's knit in a big gauge with a simple stitch. Second, the button bands are knit in place in the front and extend around to join in back—no pick-up-and-knit bands! Third, it will work with just about any yarn. With its simple shape and subtle texture, this pattern works well with a complex novelty yarn, as shown in the model sweater. Or, make your own novelty yarn! Just combine two or three thin, complementary yarns for a great new look. Or go casual with a textured solid. But maybe most important, this sweater is very easy to wear. With its long, slimming look, it can work for office, evening, or a walk in the woods!

LEFT

Sample knit with two strands of S. Charles Ritratto (28% mohair, 53% rayon, 10% nylon, 9% polyester; 50 g, 180 m per skein) with one strand of Trendsetter Yarns Sunshine (75% rayon, 25% nylon; 50 g, 85 m per skein) on #13 needles.

Sample gauge: 11 sts and 16 rows = 4" in patt

BOTTOM LEFT

Sample knit in Mission Falls 1824 Cotton (100% cotton; 50 g, 84 yds per skein) on #9 needles.

Sample gauge: 15 sts and 22 rows = 4" in patt

Yarn Required (in yards)

Finished Sweater Size	33"	36"	40"	44"	48"
Gauge (No. sts = 4")			Yards		
10			875	950	1,050
11		875	1,000	1,100	1,200
12	850	975	1,125	1,225	1,350
13	950	1,075	1,250	1,350	
14	1,025	1,175	1,325	1,500	
15	1,125	1,275	1,475		

Additional Materials

✦ Needles, the size used for gauge swatch

✦ 5 buttons (or desired number)

Before You Begin:

1. Make a gauge swatch in the Triple Rib pattern. This sweater can be made in gauges of 10–15 stitches = 4" (chunky range).

2. Determine the sweater size that you want to make (see page 10).

3. Identify the pattern number that will produce the sweater size that you want (see pages 10–12). Directions are given for pattern number 1; changes for pattern numbers 2, 3, 4, and 5 are in parentheses. Note that a pattern number 1 does not necessarily mean a 33" sweater size!

4. Review the sweater measurements in the table below. The letters in the table correspond to the letters on the diagrams. Adjust lengths as necessary for the fit that you want.

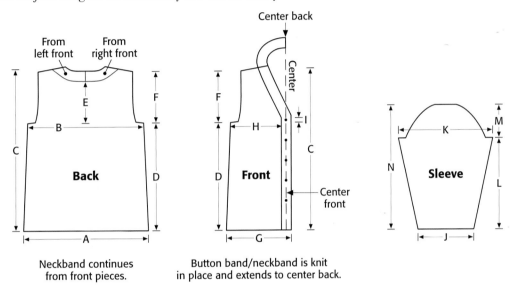

Neckband continues from front pieces.

Button band/neckband is knit in place and extends to center back.

Sweater Measurements (in inches)

Finished Sweater Size	33	36	40	44	48
A. Back width (at bottom)	18	20	22	24	26
B. Back width (at bust)	16½	18	20	22	24
C. Back length, front length (not including neckband)	26	27½	29	29½	30
D. Length to armhole	18	19	20	20	20
E. Length from armhole to back neck	6	6½	7	7½	8
F. Length from armhole to shoulder	8	8½	9	9½	10
G. Front width (at bottom)	10½	10½	12½	12½	14
H. Front width (at bust)	10	10	12	12	13½
I. Length from armhole to front neck	1½	1½	2	2	2
J. Sleeve width at cuff	8	9	9	10	10
K. Sleeve width at underarm	14½	15½	16½	18	19
L. Sleeve length to underarm	15½	17	17	17	17
M. Length of sleeve cap	5	5½	6	6½	6½
N. Total sleeve length	20½	22½	23	23½	23½

Back

1. CO 53 (59, 65, 71, 77) sts. Work in Triple Rib patt for about 7", dec 1 st at each side. At about 14", dec 1 st at each side—49 (55, 61, 67, 73) sts rem.

2. At measurement D, beg armhole shaping: BO 3 sts at beg of next 2 rows. Dec 1 st at each side next 3 RS rows—37 (43, 49, 55, 61) sts rem.

3. At measurement E, beg back neck shaping: Work across 13 (14, 16, 17, 20) sts, join second ball of yarn, BO center 11 (15, 17, 21, 21) sts, finish row. Working both sides at same time, at each neck edge, BO 2 (2, 2, 3, 3) sts; 2 rows later, BO 1 (2, 2, 2, 3) sts; 2 rows later, BO 1 (1, 2, 2, 2) sts.

4. AT SAME TIME, at measurement F, BO rem 9 (9, 10, 10, 12) sts on each shoulder.

Front

1. For each front, CO 31 (31, 37, 37, 43) sts. Work in Triple Rib patt with following change: At center edge, expand the 3 sts (K1, P1, K1) to 5 sts (K1, P1, K1, P1, K1 on RS, P5 on WS). This 5-st rib (plus the selvage st for a sixth st) will be the button band.

2. At 4 (5, 6, 6, 6)", make first buttonhole in right side button band (see "Buttonholes," page 135). Space buttonholes every 3½" for a total of 5 buttonholes; top buttonhole will be even with start of the armhole shaping.

3. AT SAME TIME, at about 9", dec 1 st at side edge. Rep at about 16"—29 (29, 35, 35, 41) sts rem.

4. AT SAME TIME, at measurement D, work armhole shaping as for back—23 (23, 29, 29, 35) sts rem.

5. AT SAME TIME, at measurement I, beg front neck shaping: Dec 1 st just inside button band (on both right and left sides) 7 (7, 12, 12, 16) times between measurements G and E.

6. AT SAME TIME, at measurement F, BO 9 (9, 10, 10, 12) sts from shoulder edge—7 sts rem (5-st rib of button band, plus 2 selvage sts).

7. Cont working (what is now) the 7-st back neckband in patt as follows:

   Row 1 (RS): KS, K1, P1, K1, P1, K1, KS.
   Row 2 (WS): KS, P5, KS.

   To make curve, alternate pairs of short rows (see page 135) on outside 4 sts on sweater edge with pairs of full rows. Work until bands are long enough to meet in center back. For best result, baste back piece in place at shoulder and baste neckband to back piece as you knit. BO.

Neckband

1. Sew permanent shoulder seams.

2. Sew back neckbands to back neck. Sew neckbands together at center back.

Sleeves

1. For each sleeve, CO 25 (29, 29, 31, 31) sts. Work sizes 1, 4, and 5 in Triple Rib with Border patt. Work sizes 2 and 3 in Triple Rib patt. Inc 1 st at each side 9 (9, 10, 12, 13) times, evenly spaced between beg and measurement L—43 (47, 49, 55, 57) sts.

2. At measurement L, beg sleeve cap: BO 4 (4, 4, 5, 5) sts at beg of next 2 rows. Dec 1 st at each side of each RS row until sleeve cap measures 4½ (4½, 4½, 5, 5½)". BO 2 sts at beg of each row until sleeve cap reaches measurement M. BO rem sts.

And Finally

Sew in sleeves. Sew side seams, leaving bottom 6" open. Sew sleeve seams. Sew on buttons.

Soft-Twist Tunic

This sweater can be made in gauges of 20–25 stitches = 4" (DK range).

Model sweater knit in Karabella Yarns Gossamer (30% kid mohair, 52% nylon, 18% polyester; 50 g, 200 m per skein) on #9 needles.

Model gauge: 21 sts and 21 rows = 4" in soft twist patt

The Soft-Twist Tunic is designed for a lightweight fabric. The bottom of the sweater is ribbed, and nine-stitch cables are worked in a staggered pattern to pull the fabric in and create the A-line shape. Long, finger-length sleeves with cabled cuffs and a deep V-neck complete the delicate shaping. Feel free to play with the placement of the cable twists. Make them more staggered or more aligned. For a great maternity look, start them all at the same time at the armhole shaping.

Look for a lightweight yarn (150 to 250 yards for 50 grams). A soft mohair yarn is a great choice here, or think about a light ribbon. Expect to use needles a few sizes up from the recommended size. Also make sure the fabric feels right; it should be as soft and light as a cloud!

RIGHT

Sample knit in Artfibers Papyrus (100% mercerized cotton ribbon; 50 g, 127 yds per skein) on #9 needles. Sample gauge: 22 sts and 24 rows = 4" in Soft Twist pattern

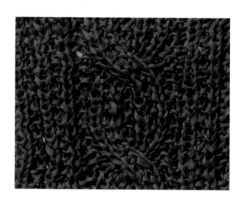

Yarn Required (in yards)

Finished Sweater Size	33"	36"	40"	44"	48"
Gauge (No. sts = 4")			Yards		
20		1,725	1,975	2,150	2,300
21	1,625	1,825	2,075	2,275	2,450
22	1,675	1,925	2,200	2,400	2,575
23	1,750	2,025	2,325	2,525	2,700
24	1,850	2,125	2,425	2,650	
25	1,925	2,225	2,550	2,775	

Additional Materials

✦ Needles, the size used for gauge swatch

✦ Cable needle

Before You Begin:

1. Make a gauge swatch in the Soft Twist pattern. This sweater can be made in gauges of 20–25 stitches = 4" (DK range).

2. Determine the sweater size that you want to make (see page 10).

3. Identify the pattern number that will produce the sweater size that you want (see pages 10–12). Directions are given for pattern number 1; changes for pattern numbers 2, 3, 4, and 5 are in parentheses. Note that a pattern number 1 does not necessarily mean a 33" sweater size!

4. Review the sweater measurements in the table below. The letters in the table correspond to the letters on the diagrams. Adjust lengths as necessary for the fit that you want.

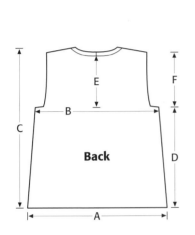

Narrow neckband continues
from front piece.

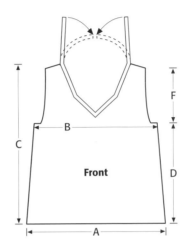

Neckband extensions are knit
straight out from front shoulder
and sewn down to curve of back neck.

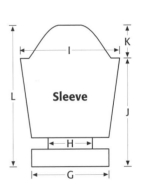

Sweater Measurements (in inches)

Finished Sweater Size	33	36	40	44	48
A. Back width, front width (at bottom, before cable twists)	23	25	28	31	33
B. Back width, front width (at bust)	16½	18	20	22	24
C. Back length, front length (not including neckband)	24½	26	27½	28	28½
D. Length to armhole	15½	16½	17½	17½	17½
E. Length from armhole to back neck	8	8½	9	9½	10
F. Length from armhole to shoulder	8½	9	9½	10	10½
G. Sleeve width before cuff	11½	11½	14	14	14
H. Sleeve width at cuff	9	9	11	11	11
I. Sleeve width at underarm	14	15	16	17½	19
J. Sleeve length to underarm	17½	18½	19	19	19
K. Length of sleeve cap	5	5½	6	6½	6½
L. Total sleeve length	22½	24	25	25½	25½

Back

T9 = Twist 9 sts: Sl 6 sts to cn and hold at front, work next 3 sts as (K1, P1, K1), sl 3 sts from cn back to left needle and work as (P1, K1, P1), work last 3 sts from cn as (K1, P1, K1).

1. CO 95 (103, 107, 119, 131) sts. Sizes 1, 3, 4, and 5: Work in Triple Rib patt. Size 2: Work in Triple Rib with Border patt. Work to about 4½ (5½, 6½, 6½, 6½)". Work Triple Rib patt across 19 (23, 25, 31, 37) sts, T9, work in patt across 39 sts, T9, work in patt to end of row. Sixteen rows later, work in patt across 19 (23, 25, 31, 37) sts, T9, work in patt across 15 sts, T9, work in patt across 15 sts, T9, work to end of row. Sixteen rows later, beg Soft Twist chart on facing page. For sizes 1, 2, and 3, work 7 (11, 13, 0, 0) sts in Triple Rib patt as established, start Soft Twist chart at row 9, work 24-st rep 3 times, work final cable sts as indicated on chart, work rem 7 (11, 13, 0, 0) sts in Triple Rib patt. For sizes 4 and 5, work 0 (0, 0, 7, 13) sts in Triple Rib patt, start chart at row 1, work 24-st rep 4 times, work final cable sts as indicated on chart, work rem 0 (0, 0, 7, 13) sts in Triple Rib patt.

2. At measurement D, beg armhole shaping: BO 2 (2, 4, 2, 6) sts at beg of next 2 rows. Dec 1 st at each side next 2 (2, 2, 2, 4) RS rows—87 (95, 95, 111, 111) sts. Note that the different sizes have different edges:

    For size 1, edge with (KS, K1, P1) on outside of first and last (7th) cable.

    For sizes 2 and 3, edge with KS, 6 sts of Triple Rib on outside of first and last (7th) cable.

    For sizes 4 and 5, edge with (KS, K1, P1) on outside of first and last (9th) cable.

3. At measurement E, beg back neck shaping: Work across 29 (31, 31, 37, 37) sts, join second ball of yarn, BO center 29 (33, 33, 37, 37) sts, finish row. Working both sides at same time, at each neck edge, BO 4 (4, 4, 5, 5) sts; 2 rows later, BO 4 (4, 4, 5, 5) sts; 2 rows later, BO 3 (4, 4, 5, 5) sts.

4. AT SAME TIME, at measurement F, beg shoulder shaping: At each shoulder edge, BO 6 (6, 6, 7, 7) sts; 2 rows later, BO 6 (7, 7, 8, 8) sts; 2 rows later, BO rem 6 (6, 6, 7, 7) sts.

Front

1. Work as for back to measurement D. Work armhole shaping as for back.

2. AT SAME TIME, work until 4th cable cross of center cable (approx 1" above armhole). Next WS row, dec 1 st at center. Next RS row, work to center cable (which now has 8 sts). Work first 4 sts as (K1, P1, K1, KS). These 4 sts are now the left front neckband. Join second ball of yarn. Work rem sts of center cable as (KS, K1, P1, K1) (the right front neckband). Cont in patt, working 2 front sides separately—43 (47, 47, 55, 55) sts each side.

3. AT SAME TIME, dec 1 st (just inside neckband) at each neck edge next 10 RS rows. Dec 1 st at each neck edge 10 (13, 13, 18, 18) more times, evenly spaced to measurement F.

4. AT SAME TIME, at measurement F, beg shoulder shaping: At each shoulder edge, BO 6 (6, 6, 7, 7) sts; 2 rows later, BO 6 (7, 7, 8, 8) sts; 2 rows later, BO 6 (6, 6, 7, 7) sts. Cont working rem 5 sts as (KS, K1, P1, K1, KS) until neckbands are long enough to meet in center back.

Neck Finishing

1. Sew permanent shoulder seams.

2. Sew neckbands to back neck. Sew neckbands together at center back.

Sleeves

1. For each sleeve, CO 47 (47, 59, 59, 59) sts. Work in Triple Rib patt for 3"; then work Cable Cuff chart for 12 rows.

2. Cont in Triple Rib patt, inc 1 st at each side 10 (14, 13, 16, 19) times, evenly spaced between top of cuff and measurement J—67 (75, 85, 91, 97) sts.

3. At measurement J, beg sleeve cap: BO 4 (4, 5, 5, 6) sts at beg of next 2 rows. Dec 1 st at each side of each RS row until sleeve cap measures 4½ (4½, 4½, 5, 5½)". BO 2 sts at beg of each row until sleeve cap reaches measurement K. BO rem sts.

And Finally

1. Sew in sleeves.

2. Sew side seams (with vent if desired) and sleeve seams.

Soft Twist Pattern

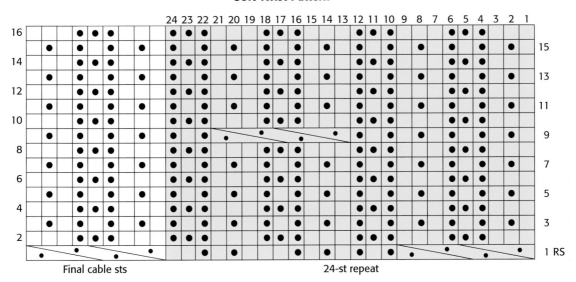

Final cable sts 24-st repeat

Cable Cuff Pattern

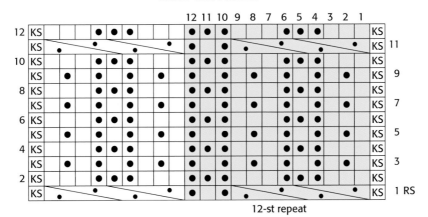

12-st repeat

KS	Knit selvage
	K on RS, P on WS
●	P on RS, K on WS

Sl 6 sts to cn and hold in front, work next 3 sts as K1, P1, K1, sl 3 sts back to left needle and work as P1, K1, P1, work last 3 sts from cn as K1, P1, K1.

Shawl and Scarf

*T*he Triple Rib stitch is ideal for putting just enough texture into a simple scarf or shawl. Find a great, soft yarn (or combination of yarns) that will knit up to a nice texture on great-big needles. In the shawl, a featherlight, superkid mohair blend is combined with a black nylon ribbon to add a little body and shine. In the scarf, a ribbon with a little shine and subtle variegation makes an all-occasion accessory.

Before you begin, make a gauge swatch. The shawl is designed for a super-chunky gauge range of 8 to 10 stitches over 4". Also make sure the fabric feels right. It should be soft and light. The scarf can be worked in super-chunky or chunky gauge (8 to 15 stitches over 4"). Scarves and shawls stretch a lot, so when you're measuring gauge here, stretch your swatch out quite a bit.

Materials for Shawl

Yarn Required (in yards)	
Gauge (No sts = 4")	Yards
8	600
9	700
10	800

Additional Materials

✦ Needles, the size used for gauge swatch

✦ Crochet hook for fringe

Directions

Directions are given for a gauge of 8 sts over 4". Changes for gauges 9 and 10 sts over 4" are in parentheses.

Shawl

This shawl can be made in gauges of 8–10 stitches = 4".

Finished size (before fringe) approx 24" x 72".

Model shawl knit in Artfibers Santorini (superkid mohair, cotton, tactel; 50 g, 174 yds per skein) with Fonty Serpentine (100% nylon; 50 g, 130 m per skein) on #17 needles.

Model gauge: 8 sts and 10 rows = 4" with knitting stretched

1. Before beg, cut yarn for fringe: 94 (106, 118) strands, approx 18" long. If you're working with 2 or more yarns held together, use the same combination in the fringe. Set aside.

2. CO 47 (53, 59) sts. Work in Triple Rib patt to about 72" or desired length. BO loosely.

3. Attach fringe: Fold one strip of yarn (or combination of yarns) at center. Using crochet hook, pull about 4" of folded yarn through first row of first st. Pull tail of yarn through folded end. Tighten. Rep for all sts at each end.

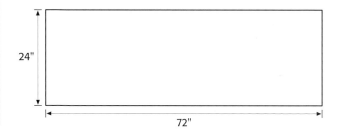

Scarf

This scarf can be made in gauges of 8–15 stitches = 4".

Finished size approx 7" x 60".

Model scarf knit in Colinette Yarns Giotto (50% cotton, 40% rayon, 10% nylon; 100 g, 144 m per skein) on #11 needles.

Model gauge: 12 sts and 12 rows = 4" with knitting stretched

Materials for Scarf

Yarn Required (in yards)

Gauge (No sts = 4")	Yards
8	175
9	200
10	225
11	250
12–13	300
14–15	350

Additional Materials

Needles, the size used for gauge swatch

Directions

1. For all gauges, CO 5 sts. Work 2 rows Triple Rib patt (Row 1: KS, K1, P1, K1; KS Row 2: KS, P3, KS). Next RS row, inc 1 st at each side. Inc 1 st at each side each RS row until work is about 7" wide.

2. Work to about 55" long. Next RS row, dec 1 st at each side. Dec 1 st at each side each RS row until 5 sts rem. BO loosely.

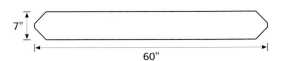

7"   60"

Cascading Leaves

One day, my then nine-year-old daughter asked for a new sweater, so we made a trip to our local yarn shop. She quickly fell in love with a variegated mohair in the colors of peach and raspberry. I warned her that mohair was very warm for our northern California climate, and that it was probably too scratchy to wear next to her skin. She wasn't swayed, and we brought it home.

When I think of mohair, I think of cables and lace. The Cascading Leaves pattern is a perfect choice. It's a very simple pattern—there are no actual cable twists. The slanted stitches are made by increasing on one side of a pair of stitches and decreasing on the other side. These slanted stitches become the outlines of the leaves. Using yarn overs for the increases creates a pattern of lacy open spaces. It was a great marriage of yarn and stitch, and before long, my daughter was wearing the Rolled Neck Pullover.

The sweaters in this chapter feature the Cascading Leaves pattern, plus two variations. One variation, Leaves and Stem, is a pattern of alternating leaves climbing up a stem. The second, designed for narrow areas and/or big-gauge yarns, highlights one column of leaves at a time. As shown with a wide range of yarns, the stitch can take you from glittery formal styles to super-warm bulk or anywhere in between. You decide!

Tips

Decreases: Each stitch pattern includes two types of decreases. The pattern will not look right unless the right decrease stitch is used. For stitches that slant up to the right, work K2tog. For stitches that slant up to the left, work sl 1 kw, K1, psso.

Binding off: The bind off will look tidier if you work the first 2 stitches and last 2 stitches of each Cascading Leaves pattern together. If you are working them on the wrong side, purl the first 2 stitches together and the last 2 stitches together. On the right side, knit the first 2 stitches together. For the last 2, sl 1, K1, and psso.

Pattern size: To make the stitch work across multiple pattern sizes, two techniques are used (sometimes together!). One is to vary the number of pattern repeats in different sizes. The second is to change the number of stitches in the pattern.

Holes: Each of these patterns features yarn overs to create a lacy effect; that is, they have holes in them. If you prefer a sweater without holes, try substituting a "make 1" for "yarn over" in the pattern charts. Check the gauge carefully; it will be a bit different.

Leaf-Print Shell

This sweater can be made in gauges of 15–20 stitches = 4" (worsted range).
Model sweater knit in Online Nobile (75% acrylic, 16% cupro, 9% polyester;
50 g, 90 m per skein) on #10½ needles.
Model gauge: 16 sts and 24 rows = 4" in patt

This shell features a variation on the leaf pattern that looks like alternating leaves climbing up a stem. As shown on the model in an elegant metallic yarn, it's ready for a trip to the opera or a holiday party. For a more casual look, try a smooth or brushed yarn, or try something a little fuzzy.

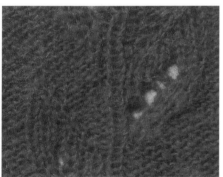

LEFT

Sample knit in Classic Elite Yarns Premiere (50% pima cotton, 50% tencel; 50 g, 108 yds per skein) on #6 needles.

Sample gauge: 18 sts and 26 rows = 4" in patt

BOTTOM LEFT

Sample knit in Artfibers Whisper (63% superkid mohair, 20% nylon, 17% extra fine wool; 50 g, 193 yds per skein) on #8 needles.

Sample gauge: 15 sts and 24 rows = 4" in patt

Yarn Required (in yards)

Finished Sweater Size	33"	36"	40"	44"	48"
Gauge (No. sts = 4")			Yards		
15		525	600	675	725
16	450	575	650	725	775
17	500	625	700	775	850
18	525	675	750	825	
19	575	700	800	875	
20	600	750	850		

Additional Materials

✦ Needles, the size used for gauge swatch

✦ Crochet hook, the size specified for yarn

Before You Begin:

1. Make a gauge swatch in the Leaves and Stem pattern. This sweater can be made in gauges of 15–20 stitches = 4" (worsted range).

2. Determine the sweater size that you want to make (see page 10).

3. Identify the pattern number that will produce the sweater size that you want (see pages 10–12). Directions are given for pattern number 1; changes for pattern numbers 2, 3, 4, and 5 are in parentheses. Note that a pattern number 1 does not necessarily mean a 33" sweater size!

4. Review the sweater measurements in the table below. The letters in the table correspond to the letters on the diagrams. Adjust lengths as necessary for the fit that you want.

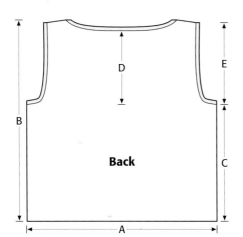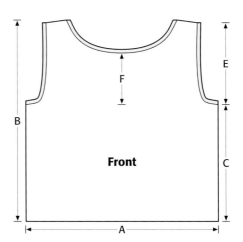

Narrow crocheted edges are added later.

Sweater Measurements (in inches)

Finished Sweater Size	33	36	40	44	48
A. Back width, front width	16½	18	20	22	24
B. Back length, front length	16½	18	19	19½	20
C. Length to armhole	10	11	11½	11½	11½
D. Length from armhole to back neck	5½	6	6½	7	7½
E. Length from armhole to shoulder	6½	7	7½	8	8½
F. Length from armhole to front neck	4	4½	5	5½	6

Back

1. CO 71 (78, 86, 95, 103) sts. Work in patt as follows (see Leaves and Stem [LS15] chart at right):

   Size 1: KS, P9, LS15, P3, LS15, P3, LS15, P9, KS.

   Size 2: KS, P5, LS15, P2, LS15, P2, LS15, P2, LS15, P5, KS.

   Size 3: KS, P9, LS15, P2, LS15, P2, LS15, P2, LS15, P9, KS.

   Size 4: KS, P12, LS15, P3, LS15, P3, LS15, P3, LS15, P12, KS.

   Size 5: KS, P13, LS15, P5, LS15, P5, LS15, P5, LS15, P13, KS.

   On WS, work all sts as presented.

2. At measurement C, beg armhole shaping: BO 4 (2, 4, 6, 6) sts at beg of next 2 rows. Dec 1 st at each side next 5 (3, 5, 6, 7) RS rows—53 (68, 68, 71, 77) sts.

3. At measurement D, beg back neck shaping: Work across 16 (21, 21, 22, 24) sts, join second ball of yarn, BO center 21 (26, 26, 27, 29) sts, finish row. Working both sides at same time, at each neck edge: BO 4 (5, 5, 5, 6) sts; 2 rows later, BO 4 (6, 6, 6, 6) sts.

4. AT SAME TIME, at measurement E, BO rem 8 (10, 10, 11, 12) sts for each shoulder.

Front

1. Work as for back, steps 1–2. At measurement F, beg front neck shaping: Work across 18 (24, 24, 25, 26) sts, join second ball of yarn, BO center 17 (20, 20, 21, 25) sts, finish row. Working both sides at same time, at each neck edge, BO 3 (5, 5, 5, 5) sts; 2 rows later, BO 3 (5, 5, 5, 5) sts; dec 1 st 4 times.

2. AT SAME TIME, at measurement E, work shoulder shaping as for back.

Neckband

1. Sew permanent seams in both shoulders.

2. Work a single crochet edge around neck, beg and ending at center back (see "Crocheted Edges," page 140).

And Finally

1. Sew permanent side seams.

2. Work a single crochet edge around both armholes, beg and ending at side seam.

Leaves and Stem (LS15)

15-st repeat

●	P on RS, K on WS	
□	K on RS, P on WS	
◹	SKP (sl 1 kw, K1, psso)	
◺	K2tog	
M	Make 1 st as to purl	
O	Yarn over	

Rolled-Neck Pullover

This sweater can be made in gauges of 15–20 stitches = 4" (worsted range).

Model sweater knit in di. Ve Mohair Kiss Ombre (73% mohair, 22% wool, 5% nylon; 50 g, 90 m per skein) on #8 needles.

Model gauge: 17 sts and 23 rows = 4" in patt

This sweater was designed with mohair in mind. Fuzzy yarns are terrific with open-space patterns. To keep the potentially scratchy fabric away from the skin, the neckline features a rolled collar, and the sleeves are wide and loose. Feel free to experiment with yarn texture here. Smooth yarns will show off every stitch. Fuzzy yarns, such as a light bouclé, will soften the look. Both are beautiful.

LEFT

Sample knit in GGH Lamour (50% extrafine wool, 33% angora, 17% nylon; 25 g, 80 m per skein) on #7 needles.

Sample gauge: 16 sts and 26 rows = 4" in patt

BOTTOM LEFT

Sample knit in Silver Creek Yarn Co. Superwash Merino Tencel (43% merino wool, 42% tencel, 15% polyester; skein sizes vary; approx 92 yds per oz) on #7 needles.

Sample gauge: 15 sts and 22 rows = 4" in patt

Yarn Required (in yards)

Finished Sweater Size	33"	36"	40"	44"	48"
Gauge (No. sts = 4)			Yards		
15		1,075	1,225	1,375	1,525
16	1,000	1,150	1,325	1,475	1,650
17	1,075	1,250	1,425	1,600	1,775
18	1,150	1,325	1,525	1,700	
19	1,225	1,425	1,625	1,825	
20	1,300	1,500	1,725		

Additional Materials

Needles, the size used for gauge swatch

Before You Begin:

1. Make a gauge swatch in the Cascading Leaves (CL14) pattern. This sweater can be made in gauges of 15–20 stitches = 4" (worsted range).

2. Determine the sweater size that you want to make (see page 10).

3. Identify the pattern number that will produce the sweater size that you want (see pages 10–12). Directions are given for pattern number 1; changes for pattern numbers 2, 3, 4, and 5 are in parentheses. Note that a pattern number 1 does not necessarily mean a 33" sweater size!

4. Review the sweater measurements in the table below. The letters in the table correspond to the letters on the diagrams. Adjust lengths as necessary for the fit that you want.

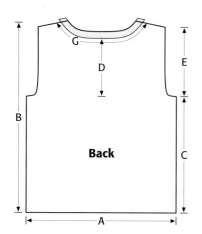

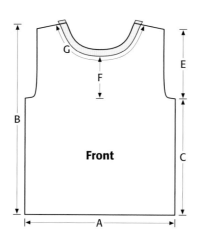

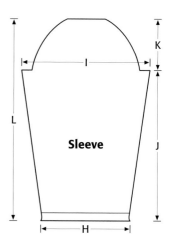

Measurement G is the inside of the collar, back and front.
Rolled neckband is added later and rolls
to the outside, about 1½" total depth.

Bottom of sleeve rolls to the front,
but should be flattened to measure.

Sweater Measurements (in inches)

Finished Sweater Size	33	36	40	44	48
A. Back width, front width	16½	18	20	22	24
B. Back length, front length	20	22	23	23½	24½
C. Length to armhole	12	13½	14	14	14
D. Length from armhole to back neck	6	6½	7	7½	8½
E. Length from armhole to shoulder	7½	8	8½	9	10
F. Length from armhole to front neck	4½	5	5½	6	7
G. Collar length	20	21	22	23	24
H. Sleeve width at cuff	9	10	11	12	12½
I. Sleeve width at underarm	14	15	16	17	19
J. Sleeve length to underarm*	16½	17½	18	18	18
K. Length of sleeve cap	5	5½	6	6½	6½
L. Total sleeve length*	21½	23	24	24½	24½

*When measuring sleeve length, uncurl rolled cuff edges.

Back

1. CO 72 (76, 86, 95, 104) sts. Work in patt as follows (see Cascading Leaves [CL] charts, page 106):

   Size 1: KS, K4, P5, CL14, P5, CL14, P5, CL14, P5, K4, KS.

   Size 2: KS, K4, P6, CL14, P6, CL14, P6, CL14, P6, K4, KS.

   Size 3: KS, K6, P6, CL16, P6, CL16, P6, CL16, P6, K6, KS.

   Size 4: KS, K6, P5, CL14, P5, CL14, P5, CL14, P5, CL14, P5, K6, KS.

   Size 5: KS, K8, P6, CL14, P6, CL14, P6, CL14, P6, CL14, P6, K8, KS.

   On WS, work all sts as presented.

2. At measurement C, beg armhole shaping: BO 3 (3, 4, 4, 5) sts at beg of next 2 rows. Dec 1 st at each side next 4 (4, 5, 5, 6) RS rows—58 (62, 68, 77, 82) sts. Work in patt as follows:

   Size 1: KS, P2, CL14, P5, CL14, P5, CL14, P2, KS.

   Size 2: KS, P3, CL14, P6, CL14, P6, CL14, P3, KS.

   Size 3: KS, P3, CL16, P6, CL16, P6, CL16, P3, KS.

   Size 4: KS, P2, CL14, P5, CL14, P5, CL14, P5, CL14, P2, KS.

   Size 5: KS, P3, CL14, P6, CL14, P6, CL14, P6, CL14, P3, KS.

3. Work to measurement D, ending with completed RS row. In next (WS) row, work first 2 sts tog on CL patt that is closest to the center and work last 2 sts tog on CL patt that is closest to center. Next row, work across 20 (22, 23, 26, 28) sts, move center 16 (16, 20, 23, 24) sts to holder, join second ball of yarn, finish row. Working both sides at same time, at each neck edge: BO 2 (3, 4, 4, 4) sts; 2 rows later, BO 2 (3, 3, 4, 4) sts; dec 1 st next 2 RS rows.

4. AT SAME TIME, at measurement E, beg shoulder shaping: At each shoulder edge, BO 7 (7, 7, 8, 9) sts; 2 rows later, BO rem 7 (7, 7, 8, 9) sts. When binding off, work first 2 sts and last 2 sts of each CL patt tog.

Front

1. Work as for back, steps 1–2. At measurement F, ending with completed RS row, beg front neck shaping: In next row (WS), work first 2 sts tog in CL patt that is closest to center and work last 2 sts tog in CL patt that is closest to center. Next row, work across 22 (24, 25, 29, 31) sts, move center 12 (12, 16, 17, 18) sts to holder, join second ball of yarn, finish row. Working both sides at once, at each neck edge BO 2 (2, 3, 4, 4) sts; 2 rows later, BO 2 (2, 2, 3, 3) sts; 2 rows later, BO 0 (2, 2, 2, 2) sts; dec 1 st next 4 RS rows.

2. AT SAME TIME, at measurement E, work shoulder shaping as for back.

Collar

1. Sew permanent seam in one shoulder.

2. For collar: Multiply measurement G by st-per-inch gauge. PU approx this number of sts, a bit more than half from the front. (The total number will range from about 75 for a small size in a big gauge to 120 for a large size in a small gauge.) Work in St st so RS of stitch is on RS of sweater. Work for approx 1½". BO loosely. Remember that collar will curl forward and reverse St st will show on outside of sweater collar.

3. Sew permanent seam in second shoulder, including collar.

Sleeves

1. For each sleeve, CO 38 (42, 46, 50, 54) sts. Work in St st for approx 1", ending with completed purl row. The WS of fabric will curl to outside of sleeve.

2. Work in patt as follows:

   Size 1: KS, P11, CL14, P11, KS.

   Size 2: KS, P13, CL14, P13, KS.

   Size 3: KS, P14, CL16, P14, KS.

   Size 4: KS, P17, CL14, P17, KS.

   Size 5: KS, P19, CL14, P19, KS.

   On WS, work all sts as presented.

3. Inc 1 st at each side 10 (10, 11, 12, 13) times, evenly spaced between top of cuff and measurement J—58 (62, 68, 74, 80) sts.

4. At measurement J, beg sleeve cap: BO 4 (4, 5, 5, 6) sts at beg of next 2 rows. Dec 1 st at each side of each RS row until sleeve cap measures 4½ (4½, 4½, 5, 5½)". BO 2 sts at beg of each row until sleeve cap reaches measurement K. BO rem sts.

And Finally

1. Sew in sleeves.

2. Sew side seams and sleeve seams.

14-st Cascading Leaves (CL14)

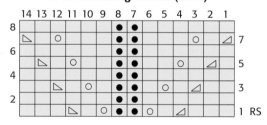

16-st Cascading Leaves (CL16)

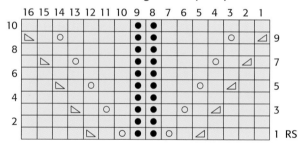

- ● P on RS, K on WS
- ☐ K on RS, P on WS
- ◿ SKP (sl 1 kw, K1, psso)
- ◺ K2tog
- ○ Yarn over

Bold Leaf Jacket

This sweater can be made in gauges of 8–10 stitches = 4" (super chunky range).

Model sweater knit in Cleckheaton Gusto 10 (30% wool, 30% mohair, 40% acrylic; 100 g, 51 m per skein) on #15 needles.

Model gauge: 9 sts and 12 rows = 4" in patt

*W*hat do you do with a super-chunky yarn? Make a great, warm jacket! For maximum drama, the Split Leaf design is blown up to a bold scale. I love this type of "faux" cable pattern in a super-chunky yarn. It gives the effect of cables without the thickened regions of crossed stitches. To see every detail of every stitch, choose a smooth, light-colored yarn as shown in the model sweater. Or not! How about the intriguing stitch definition of a big, thick/thin yarn in a bold variegated color scheme?

RIGHT

Sample knit in Gedifra Gigante (100% new wool; 50 g, 30 m per skein) on #13 needles.

Sample gauge: 10 sts and 15 rows = 4" in patt

Yarn Required (in yards)

Finished Sweater Size	33"	36"	40"	44"	48"
Gauge (No. sts = 4")			Yards		
8		525	575	625	675
9	525	625	675	750	800
10	600	725	800	850	

Additional Materials

✦ Needles, the size used for gauge swatch

✦ 7 buttons (or number desired)

Before You Begin:

1. Make a gauge swatch in the Split Leaf (SLR9) pattern. This sweater can be made in gauges of 8–10 stitches = 4" (super chunky range).

2. Determine the sweater size that you want to make (see page 10).

3. Identify the pattern number that will produce the sweater size that you want (see pages 10–12). Directions are given for pattern number 1; changes for pattern numbers 2, 3, 4, and 5 are in parentheses. Note that a pattern number 1 does not necessarily mean a 33" sweater size!

4. Review the sweater measurements in the table below. The letters in the table correspond to the letters on the diagrams. Adjust lengths as necessary for the fit that you want.

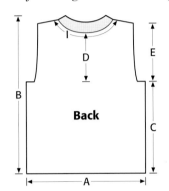 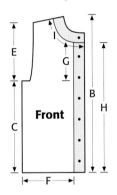 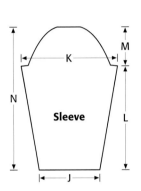

Measurement I is the length of the neckband, from center front,
around back, to center front. It includes the width of both button bands.
Neckband and button bands are added later.

Sweater Measurements (in inches)

Finished Sweater Size	33	36	40	44	48
A. Back width	16	19	20	22	25
B. Back length, front length (not including neckband)	22	23½	25	25½	26
C. Length to armhole	13	14	15	15	15
D. Length from armhole to back neck	7	7½	8	8½	9
E. Length from armhole to shoulder	8	8½	9	9½	10
F. Front width (not including button band)	7	9	9½	10	12
G. Length from armhole to front neck	4	4½	5	5½	6
H. Button band length	17	18½	20	20½	21
I. Neckband length (includes width of front button bands)	24	25	26	28	30
J. Sleeve width at cuff	9	10	10	11	11
K. Sleeve width at underarm	15½	16½	16½	17½	17½
L. Sleeve length to underarm	15	16	17	17	17
M. Length of sleeve cap	5	5½	6	6½	6½
N. Total sleeve length	20	21½	23	23½	23½

Additional abbreviations used in this sweater:

PPK5 (worked over 5 sts on RS): P2, K1, P2.

PPK8 (worked over 8 sts on RS): P2, K1, P2, K1, P2.

PPK11 (worked over 11 sts on RS): P2, K1, P2, K1, P2, K1, P2.

SLR = Split Leaf Right patt (see facing page)

SLL = Split Leaf Left patt (see facing page)

Back

1. CO 36 (44, 46, 51, 57) sts. Work in patt as follows: (see Split Leaf chart on facing page):

   Size 1: KS, K1, PPK5, SLR7, PPK8, SLL7, PPK5, K1, KS.

   Size 2: KS, K1, PPK8, SLR8, PPK8, SLL8, PPK8, K1, KS.

   Size 3: KS, K1, PPK8, SLR9, PPK8, SLL9, PPK8, K1, KS.

   Size 4: KS, K1, PPK8, SLR10, PPK11, SLL10, PPK8, K1, KS.

   Size 5: KS, K1, PPK11, SLR10, PPK11, SLL10, PPK11, K1, KS.

   On WS, work all sts as presented.

2. At measurement C, beg armhole shaping: BO 2 (3, 3, 3, 3) sts at beg of next 2 rows. Dec 1 st at each side on next 1 (3, 3, 3, 3) RS rows— 30 (32, 34, 39, 45) sts. Work in patt as follows:

   Size 1: KS, K1, P2, SLR7, PPK8, SLL7, P2, K1, KS.

   Size 2: KS, K1, P2, SLR8, PPK8, SLL8, P2, K1, KS.

   Size 3: KS, K1, P2, SLR9, PPK8, SLL9, P2, K1, KS.

   Size 4: KS, K1, P2, SLR10, PPK11, SLL10, P2, K1, KS.

   Size 5: KS, K1, PPK5, SLR10, PPK11, SLL10, PPK5, K1, KS.

3. At measurement D, beg back neck shaping. Work across 9 (10, 10, 11, 13) sts, join second ball of yarn, BO 12 (12, 14, 17, 19) sts, finish row. Working both sides at same time, dec 1 st at each neck edge next RS row.

4. AT SAME TIME, at measurement E, beg shoulder shaping: At each shoulder edge, BO 4 (4, 4, 5, 6) sts; 2 rows later, BO rem 4 (5, 5, 5, 6) sts.

Front

1. For each side, CO 18 (22, 23, 24, 27) sts. On left side, work in patt as follows (see Split Leaf chart, facing page):

   Size 1: KS, K1, PPK5, SLR7, P2, K1, KS.
   Size 2: KS, K1, PPK8, SLR8, P2, K1, KS.
   Size 3: KS, K1, PPK8, SLR9, P2, K1, KS.
   Size 4: KS, K1, PPK8, SLR10, P2, K1, KS.
   Size 5: KS, K1, PPK11, SLR10, P2, K1, KS.

   On right side, work in patt as follows:

   Size 1: KS, K1, P2, SLL7, PPK5, K1, KS.
   Size 2: KS, K1, P2, SLL8, PPK8, K1, KS.
   Size 3: KS, K1, P2, SLL9, PPK8, K1, KS.
   Size 4: KS, K1, P2, SLL10, PPK8, K1, KS.
   Size 5: KS, K1, P2, SLL10, PPK11, K1, KS.
   On WS, work all sts as presented.

2. At measurement C, work armhole shaping as for back—15 (16, 17, 18, 21) sts each side.

3. At measurement G, beg front neck shaping: At each neck edge, BO 2 (2, 3, 3, 4) sts, dec 1 st on next 5 RS rows.

4. AT SAME TIME, at measurement E, work shoulder shaping as for back.

Button Bands and Neckband

1. Sew permanent shoulder seams.

2. **Left button band:** Make gauge swatch in K1, P2 rib patt as follows: On RS rows, KS, K1, (P2, K1) across, KS. On WS rows, KS, P1, (K2, P1) across KS. Multiply st-per-inch

gauge by measurement H. PU approx this number of sts, ending with a number that is a multiple of 3. Work in patt for approx 2 (2, 2, 2½, 2½)". BO in tension that keeps button band flat and same length as sweater.

3. **Right buttonhole band:** Rep left button band, except space desired number of buttonholes in center row of band. Remember that top buttonhole will be in neckband (see "Buttonholes" on page 135).

4. **Neckband:** Multiply rib patt st-per-inch gauge by measurement I. PU approx this number of sts, ending with a number that is a multiple of 3. Work in K1, P2 rib patt for 1 (1, 1, 1¼, 1¼)". Next row P2tog 5 times evenly spaced around neckband. IN SAME ROW, make buttonhole at right neck. Working rib sts as presented, cont to 2 (2, 2, 2½, 2½)". BO in tension that allows neckband to lie flat.

Sleeves

1. For each sleeve, CO 21 (23, 23, 25, 25) sts. Work as follows (see Split Leaf chart below):

    Size 1: KS, K1, P1, SLR5, PPK5, SLL5, P1, K1, KS.

    Sizes 2 and 3: KS, K1, P2, SLR5, PPK5, SLL5, P2, K1, KS.

    Sizes 4 and 5: KS, K1, P3, SLR5, PPK5, SLL5, P3, K1, KS.

    On WS, work all sts as presented.

2. Work SLR5 and SLL5 patts for next 5 rows. Next row (WS), M1 in each Split Leaf patt. Work SLR6 and SLL 6 patts for next 7 rows. Next row (WS), M1 st in each Split Leaf patt. Work SLR7 and SLL7 patts for next 9 rows. Next row (WS), M1 st in each Split Leaf patt. Cont in SLR8 and SLL8 patts. Between this point and measurement L, M1 st at each side (just inside K1 border st) 4 times evenly spaced—35 (37, 37, 39, 39) sts. Work as follows:

    Size 1: KS, K1, P5, SLR8, PPK5, SLL8, P5, K1, KS.

    Sizes 2 and 3: KS, K1, P6, SLR8, PPK5, SLL8, P6, K1, KS.

    Sizes 4 and 5: KS, K1, P7, SLR8, PPK5, SLL8, P7, K1, KS.

3. AT SAME TIME, at measurement L, beg sleeve cap: BO 2 (2, 2, 3, 3) sts at beg of next 2 rows. Dec 1 st at each side of each RS row until sleeve cap measures 4½ (4½, 4½, 5, 5½)". BO 2 sts at beg of each row until sleeve cap reaches measurement M. BO rem sts.

And Finally

1. Sew in sleeves.

2. Sew side seams and sleeve seams using flat seams (see "Flat Seams," page 137).

3. Sew on buttons.

Left Side (SLL)

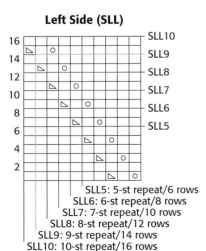

SLL5: 5-st repeat/6 rows
SLL6: 6-st repeat/8 rows
SLL7: 7-st repeat/10 rows
SLL8: 8-st repeat/12 rows
SLL9: 9-st repeat/14 rows
SLL10: 10-st repeat/16 rows

Right Side (SLR)

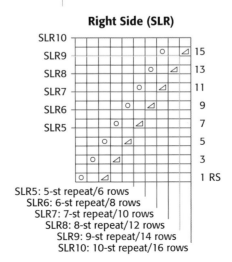

SLR5: 5-st repeat/6 rows
SLR6: 6-st repeat/8 rows
SLR7: 7-st repeat/10 rows
SLR8: 8-st repeat/12 rows
SLR9: 9-st repeat/14 rows
SLR10: 10-st repeat/16 rows

☐ K on RS, P on WS
◿ SKP (sl 1 kw, K1, psso)
◹ K2 tog
○ Yarn over

A Little Slip

There are several ways to integrate two different yarns into a fabric. You can hold two or more strands together to create a tweed effect. You can alternate yarns by row to make a wide variety of stripe effects. Or you can work two different colors in the same row, as in intarsia and Fair Isle techniques, which will yield wonderful color patterns. But my favorite method to integrate different colors is to use slip-stitch patterns.

Slip-stitch patterns range from simple to very complex. What they all share is that two or more yarns are used, but each row uses only one yarn. There are no yarns carried along the back, as in Fair Isle patterns. There are no bobbins of yarns that you find in intarsia patterns. A slip stitch is executed more like a stripe. For each pair of rows (a right-side and a wrong-side row), one yarn is used. Some of the stitches are knit (or purled) in this active yarn. Other stitches are merely slipped from the previous row. In the finished fabric, these slipped stitches are pulled up vertically. This can create flecks of color, boxes, wave patterns, or complex intarsia-like designs.

There are whole books written about slip-stitch knitting. In this book, I am starting with basic two-color slip-stitch patterns. All use two yarns. These can be different colors of the same yarn (as in the Two-Tone Tank, page 114), two coordinating yarns of similar weight (as in the Autumn Cardigan, page 126), or two wildly different yarns (as in the Tweed-Look Vest, page 118). Feel free to try any yarn combination that appeals to you. Just remember that both (or all) your yarns will be knit on the same-size needles. This is a great time to use up small amounts of yarn or yarns that are a little too daring to use alone. Go nuts!

Stitch Patterns Used in This Chapter

K1, P1 Rib
Odd number of sts
Row 1 (RS): KS, K1, (P1, K1) across, KS.
Row 2 (WS): KS, P1, (K1, P1) across, KS.
Rep rows 1 and 2.

K2, P2 Rib
Multiple of 4 plus 2
Row 1 (RS): KS, K1, (P2, K2) across, P2, K1, KS.
Row 2 (WS): KS, P1, (K2, P2) across, K2, P1, KS.
Rep rows 1 and 2.

Purl Back Rib (see page 21)

Tips

Experiment: It is hard to predict how yarns will merge in a slip stitch. When I put together the two yarns in the Plaid Sweatshirt, I intended to use them the other way—with the solid red as the main yarn and the variegated ribbon as the contrasting yarn. When I first knit a swatch that way, it looked awful! But I loved it when I switched them to what you see in the finished garment.

Mixing and matching: All of these sweaters can be made in any of the three slip-stitch patterns used in this chapter. Just make sure your stitch gauge is in the right range for the sweater pattern. The trim can be made in either the main or contrasting yarn. Note that two of the model sweaters show the trim in the main yarn and two in the contrasting yarn. Remember that the yardage numbers assume you'll use the same yarn (main or contrast) that's shown in the model sweater. Adjust your buying if you want to switch.

Using up yarns: If you want to use up small quantities of yarn, consider putting the slip-stitch pattern in selected areas of the sweaters (for example, a yoke) and fill the rest in with stockinette stitch. Alternately, consider using several different yarns in the contrasting role.

Carrying yarn: When working with two yarns, it's important to keep the tension of the unused yarn smooth up the right edge of the fabric. Try knitting the first (selvage) stitch of all right-side rows with both yarns. That keeps the loops of unused yarn from being too long (and therefore potentially too tight or too loose). On the left edge of the work, the selvage stitch is always knit in the color of the row (MC or CC). Don't try to slip the selvage stitch!

Leaving yarn behind: Binding off a few stitches (as with armhole shaping or sleeve caps) can create a minor problem. If you use only one yarn for these bind offs at the beginning of your right-side rows, you won't have the second yarn where you need it at the beginning of subsequent rows. When these bound-off stitches are on the right edge (beginning a right-side row), use both yarns for them. If that proves too bulky, try using both yarns in every second or third stitch. That way, both working yarns will be where you need them for future rows. Note that the right-side bind offs will be a little bulkier than the left.

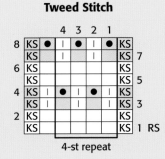

Brick Stitch

4-st repeat

Tweed Stitch

4-st repeat

Plaid Stitch

4-st repeat

KS	MC knit selvage
	MC knit on RS, purl on WS
I	MC sl st purlwise

KS	CC knit selvage
	CC knit on RS, purl on WS
●	CC knit on WS, purl on RS

Two-Tone Tank

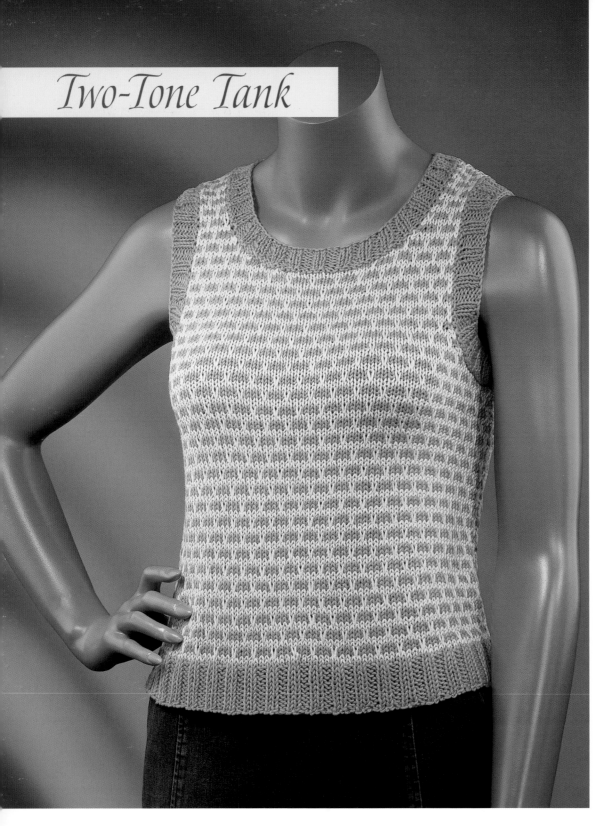

This sweater can be made in gauges of 20–25 stitches = 4" (DK range).

Model sweater knit in Brick Stitch with two shades of Dale of Norway Kolibri
(100% Egyptian cotton; 50 g, 105 m per skein) on #5 needles.

Model gauge: 22 stitches and 32 rows = 4" in patt

This sweater is shown in two colors of the same smooth cotton yarn. It is made in a basic slip-stitch pattern, the Brick Stitch. The result is a crisp, geometric pattern in a lightweight summer fabric. This can be knit in any number of colors and is a good way to use up small amounts of yarn. See how different the effect is in the Plaid or Tweed Stitch. Choose the pattern you like the best.

RIGHT

Sample knit in same yarns as on facing page, in Plaid Stitch.

BOTTOM RIGHT

Sample knit in same yarns as on facing page, in Tweed Stitch.

Yarn Required (in yards)

You will need the amount shown for both MC and CC.

Finished Sweater Size	33"	36"	40"	44"	48"
Gauge (No. sts = 4")			Yards		
20		425	475	525	600
21	400	450	500	550	625
22	425	475	525	600	650
23	450	475	550	625	700
24	475	500	575	650	
25	475	525	600	675	

Additional Materials

Needles, the size used for gauge swatch

Before You Begin:

1. Make a gauge swatch in MC an CC in the Brick Stitch pattern. This sweater can be made in gauges of 20–25 stitches = 4" (DK range).

2. Determine the sweater size that you want to make (see page 10).

3. Identify the pattern number that will produce the sweater size that you want (see pages 10–12). Directions are given for pattern number 1; changes for pattern numbers 2, 3, 4, and 5 are in parentheses. Note that a pattern number 1 does not necessarily mean a 33" sweater size!

4. Review the sweater measurements in the table below. The letters in the table correspond to the letters on the diagrams. Adjust lengths as necessary for the fit that you want.

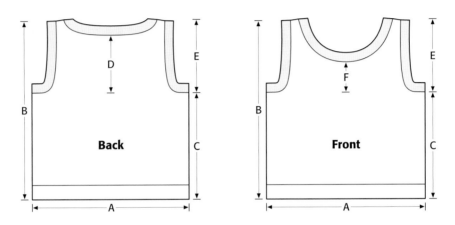

Hip band is knit in place;
neckband and armbands are added later.

Sweater Measurements (in inches)

Finished Sweater Size	33	36	40	44	48
A. Back width, front width	16½	18	20	22	24
B. Back length, front length (does not include neckband)	19½	20	20½	21	21½
C. Length to armhole (does not include armband)	11	11	11	11	11
D. Length from armhole to back neck	6½	7	7½	8	8½
E. Length from armhole to shoulder	8	8½	9	9½	10
F. Length from armhole to front neck	3½	4	4½	5	5½

Back

1. With CC, CO 90 (98, 110, 122, 134) sts. Work in K2, P2 Rib patt for 1½", ending with completed WS row. Inc 1 st in last row. Join MC and work in Brick Stitch.

2. At measurement C, beg armhole shaping: BO 7 (7, 8, 9, 10) sts at beg of next 2 rows; BO 5 (5, 6, 7, 8) sts at beg of next 2 rows; dec 1 st at each side next 4 (6, 6, 6, 6) RS rows—59 (63, 71, 79, 87) sts rem.

3. At measurement D, beg back neck shaping: Work across 23 (24, 28, 31, 34) sts, move center 13 (15, 15, 17, 19) sts to holder, join second ball of yarn, finish row. Working both sides at same time, at each neck edge, BO 3 (4, 5, 6, 6) sts; 2 rows later, BO 3 (3, 4, 4, 5) sts; 2 rows later, BO 3 (3, 3, 3, 4) sts; 2 rows later, BO 2 (2, 2, 2, 3) sts; dec 1 st next 4 RS rows.

4. AT SAME TIME, at measurement E, beg shoulder shaping: At each shoulder edge, BO 4 (4, 5, 6, 6) sts; 2 rows later, BO rem 4 (4, 5, 6, 6) sts.

Front

1. Work as for back, steps 1–2. At measurement F, beg front neck shaping: Work across 23 (24, 28, 31, 34) sts, move center 13 (15, 15, 17, 19) sts to holder, join second ball of yarn, finish row. Working both sides at same time, at each neck edge, BO 3 (4, 5, 6, 6) sts; 2 rows later, BO 3 (3, 4, 4, 5) sts; 2 rows later, BO 3 (3, 3, 3, 4) sts; 2 rows later, BO 2 (2, 2, 2, 3) sts; dec 1 st next 2 RS rows; dec 1 st every other RS row 2 times.

2. At measurement E, work shoulder shaping as for back.

Neckband

1. Put a permanent seam in one shoulder.

2. With CC, PU approx 118 (126, 134, 142, 158) sts (working sts on holders) for neckband. Inc or dec in first row to end with multiple of 4 plus 2 sts. Work in K2, P2 Rib patt for 1". BO with tension that keeps neckband curved and flat.

3. Put a permanent seam in second shoulder, including neckband. Reinforce shoulder seams if desired.

Armbands

1. With CC, PU approx 98 (106, 118, 126, 134) sts for armband. Inc or dec in first row to end with multiple of 4 plus 2 sts. Work in K2, P2 Rib patt for 1". BO with tension that keeps armband curved and flat.

2. Rep for second armband.

And Finally

1. Check tension in neckband and armbands. Tighten BO row, if necessary, to desired fit (see "Tightening a Bind-Off Row," page 133).

2. Sew side seams.

Tweed-Look Vest

This sweater can be made in gauges of 10–15 stitches = 4" (chunky range).

Model sweater knit in Mondial Class (70% wool, 30% alpaca; 100 g, 100 m per
skein) and Gedifra Gigante (100% new wool; 50 g, 30 m per skein) on
#13 needles.

Model gauge: 12 sts and 22 rows = 4" in patt

In this vest, the main yarn plays the supporting role while the star of the team is the contrasting yarn. The main yarn is a smooth, dark, chunky-weight wool-and-alpaca blend and provides a solid frame for the vest. The contrasting yarn is a big, bold, variegated, thick/thin yarn. It is exposed one stitch at a time, and every stitch is different. Try any combination of chunky yarns here. It's a great way to experiment with yarns that you might not want to wear on their own. Don't forget all those great eye-lash yarns and those soft, cuddly ones that knit up like teddy bears! They might be just the thing in a slip stitch.

RIGHT

Sample knit in Crystal Palace Yarns Merino Frappe (80% merino wool, 20% nylon; 50 g, 140 yds per skein) and Trendsetter Zucca (58% tactel, 42% nylon; 50 g, 71 yds per skein) on #11 needles.

Sample gauge: 12 sts and 24 rows = 4" in patt

Yarn Required (in yards)

Finished Sweater Size	33"	36"	40"	44"	48"
Gauge (No. sts = 4")			Yards		
10			425 MC	475 MC	500 MC
			100 CC	125 CC	125 CC
11		425 MC	450 MC	525 MC	550 MC
		100 CC	125 CC	125 CC	150 CC
12	425 MC	475 MC	500 MC	575 MC	625 MC
	100 CC	125 CC	125 CC	150 CC	175 CC
13	475 MC	525 MC	550 MC	625 MC	
	125 CC	125 CC	150 CC	175 CC	
14	525 MC	600 MC	600 MC	675 MC	
	125 CC	150 CC	150 CC	175 CC	
15	550 MC	600 MC	650 MC		
	150 CC	150 CC	175 CC		

Additional Materials

✦ Needles, the size used for gauge swatch

✦ 4 double buttons with chain; 4 regular buttons or 12" separating zipper

Before You Begin:

1. Make a gauge swatch in MC and CC in the Tweed Stitch pattern. This sweater can be made in gauges of 10–15 stitches = 4" (chunky range).

2. Determine the sweater size that you want to make (see page 10).

3. Identify the pattern number that will produce the sweater size that you want (see pages 10–12). Directions are given for pattern number 1; changes for pattern numbers 2, 3, 4, and 5 are in parentheses. Note that a pattern number 1 does not necessarily mean a 33" sweater size!

4. Review the sweater measurements in the table below. The letters in the table correspond to the letters on the diagrams. Adjust lengths as necessary for the fit that you want.

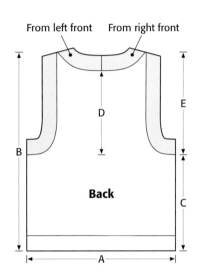

Hip band is knit in place,
armbands are added later.
Neckband continues from front pieces.

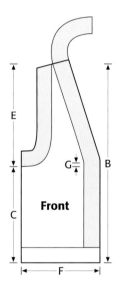

Hip band is knit in place, armbands
are added later. Button band/
neckband is worked separately
and extends to center back.

Sweater Measurements (in inches)

Finished Sweater Size	33	36	40	44	48
A. Back width	16½	18	20	22	24
B. Back length, front length (includes hip band, not neckband)	21½	22	22½	23	23½
C. Length to armhole (does not include armband)	11	11	11	11	11
D. Length from armhole to back neck	8	8½	9	9	9½
E. Length from armhole to shoulder	10½	11	11½	12	12½
F. Front width (includes button bands)	9½	10	11	12	13
G. Length from armhole to front neck	1	1	1	1	1

Back

1. With MC, CO 45 (47, 51, 57, 63) sts. Work in Purl Back Rib patt (see page 21) for 2", ending with completed WS row. Inc 6 (8, 8, 10, 10) sts evenly spaced across last row—51 (55, 59, 67, 73) sts. Join CC and work in Tweed Stitch.

2. At measurement C, beg armhole shaping: BO 4 (4, 4, 6, 6) sts at beg of next 2 rows. Dec 1 st at each side next 5 RS rows, dec 1 st at each side every other RS row 2 times—29 (33, 37, 41, 47) sts.

3. At measurement D, beg back neck shaping: Work across 12 (13, 14, 16, 18) sts, join second ball of yarn, BO center 5 (7, 9, 9, 11) sts, finish row. Working both sides at same time, at each neck edge, BO 2 (2, 3, 3, 4) sts; 2 rows later, BO 1 (2, 2, 2, 3) sts, dec 1 st next 4 RS rows. BO rem 5 (5, 5, 7, 7) sts at each shoulder.

Front

1. For each front, with MC, CO 29 (29, 31, 33, 35) sts. Work in Purl Back Rib patt for same number of rows as back hip band. Inc 3 (5, 5, 7, 7) sts evenly spaced across last row. Put 7 sts at center edge on holder. Join CC. Work rem 25 (27, 29, 33, 35) sts in Tweed Stitch.

2. At measurement C, work armhole shaping as for back—14 (16, 18, 20, 22) sts.

3. AT SAME TIME, at measurement G, beg front neck shaping: Dec 1 st at neck edge a total of 9 (11, 13, 13, 15) times, evenly spaced between measurement G and shoulder.

4. AT SAME TIME, at measurement E, BO rem 5 (5, 5, 7, 7) sts.

Neckband

1. Put a permanent seam in both shoulders. Reinforce seams if desired.

2. **Left button band:** Work sts from holder. Cont in Purl Back Rib patt until button band reaches beg of V-neck. Work pair of short rows on outside 4 sts (see "Short Rows," page 135). Cont until band is 3" short of shoulder seam. Work pair of short rows on 4 sts, on sweater side of band. Work pair of rows on all sts. Rep these last 4 rows until band reaches center back. BO.

3. **Right button band:** Work as for left button band. Add buttonholes if desired. Put lowest buttonhole in row above hip band. Put top buttonhole ½" below beg of V-neck. Space 2 or more additional buttonholes as desired (see "Buttonholes," page 135).

4. Sew button band/neckband to sweater. Sew ends of band together at center back.

Armbands

1. With MC, PU approx 71 (75, 77, 81, 83) sts for armband, ending with an odd number. Work in Purl Back Rib patt, dec 1 st at beg and end of each RS row. At 1", P3tog at lower front curve, shoulder, and lower back curve (6 st dec). At 2", BO in tension that keeps band flat. Check often to make sure finished edge lies flat; tighten or loosen tension as needed (or change needle size) to get correct tension.

2. Rep for second armband.

And Finally

1. Check tension in neckband and armbands. Tighten BO row, if necessary, to desired fit (see "Tightening a Bind-Off Row," page 133).

2. Sew side seams.

3. Sew on buttons or insert zipper. If using double buttons with chain, sew one of the chained buttons to left band and insert second chained button into buttonhole on right band.

Plaid Sweatshirt

This sweater can be made in gauges of 15–20 stitches = 4" (worsted range).

Model sweater knit in Artfibers Cairo (100% cotton ribbon; 50 g, 74 yds per skein) and Brown Sheep Company Cotton Fleece (80% cotton, 20% merino wool; 100 g, 215 yds per skein) on #9 needles.

Model gauge: 18 sts and 30 rows = 4" in patt

*H*ere's a warm and cozy sweatshirt with easy dropped shoulders and a kanga-roo pocket. It's made in a combination of great casual yarns. The main yarn is a variegated cotton ribbon in shades of red and gold. Knit in the Plaid Stitch, it creates strong vertical lines with waves of color. The contrast-ing yarn is a solid red cotton and is knit on right and wrong sides to create strong horizontal lines. Stay with soft-as-a-sweatshirt yarns or try something different! How about a monochromatic look that combines a wide ribbon with a narrow one? Invent your own plaid!

RIGHT

Sample knit in Crystal Palace Yarns Deco Rib-bon (70% acrylic, 30% nylon; 50 g, 80 yds per skein) and Jaeger Albany (100% mercerized cotton; 50 g, 105 m per skein) on #10½ needles.
Sample gauge: 16 sts and 28 rows = 4" in patt

Yarn Required (in yards)

MC is the one with slipped (elongated) sts.

Finished Sweater Size	33"	36"	40"	44"	48"
Gauge (No. sts = 4")			Yards		
15		575 MC	650 MC	700 MC	825 MC
		750 CC	825 CC	900 CC	1,000 CC
16	525 MC	600 MC	675 MC	750 MC	875 MC
	725 CC	800 CC	875 CC	950 CC	1,075 CC
17	550 MC	650 MC	725 MC	825 MC	925 MC
	775 CC	875 CC	950 CC	1,025 CC	1,150 CC
18	600 MC	700 MC	775 MC	875 MC	
	825 CC	925 CC	1,000 CC	1,100 CC	
19	625 MC	750 MC	825 MC	925 MC	
	875 CC	975 CC	1,075 CC	1,150 CC	
20	675 MC	775 MC	875 MC		
	925 CC	1,025 CC	1,125 CC		

Additional Materials

Needles, the size used for gauge swatch

Before You Begin:

1. Make a gauge swatch in MC and CC in the Plaid Stitch pattern. This sweater can be made in gauges of 15–20 stitches = 4" (worsted range).

2. Determine the sweater size that you want to make (see page 10).

3. Identify the pattern number that will produce the sweater size that you want (see pages 10–12). Directions are given for pattern number 1; changes for pattern numbers 2, 3, 4, and 5 are in parentheses. Note that a pattern number 1 does not necessarily mean a 33" sweater size!

4. Review the sweater measurements in the table below. The letters in the table correspond to the letters on the diagrams. Adjust lengths as necessary for the fit that you want.

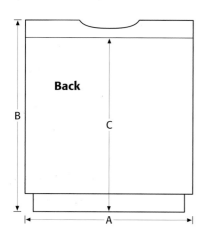

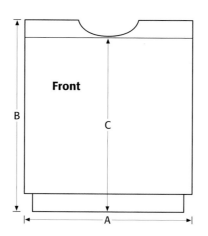

Hip band and shoulder band are knit in place;
turtleneck is added later (not shown).

Cuff is to be folded.

Sweater Measurements (in inches)

Finished Sweater Size	33	36	40	44	48
A. Back width, front width (above hip band)	16½	18	20	22	24
B. Back length, front length	20	21	22	22	23
C. Height to neckband	18	19	20	20	21
D. Sleeve width at bottom (after cuff)	10	11	11½	12	13
E. Sleeve width at underarm	15	16	17	18	20
F. Sleeve length to cap	19	20	20	21	22
G. Total sleeve length	21	22	22	23	24

Back

1. With CC, CO 61 (69, 77, 85, 93) sts. Work in K1, P1 Rib patt for 2". Inc 10 sts evenly spaced across last row—71 (79, 87, 95, 103) sts. Join MC and work in Plaid st.

2. At measurement C, switch to CC. Work in K1, P1 Rib patt for 6 rows. In row 7, work across 25 (28, 31, 34, 37) sts, move center 21 (23, 25, 27, 29) sts to holder, join second ball of yarn, finish row. Working both sides at same time, at each neck edge, dec 1 st in row 9. BO rem 24 (27, 30, 33, 36) sts with firm tension in row 11.

Front

1. Work as for back to 4". Beg kangaroo pocket: Put first 17 (19, 21, 23, 25) sts and last 17 (19, 21, 23, 25) sts on holders. Work center 37 (41, 45, 49, 53) sts for 6½". Put worked center sts on holder. Work right sts from holder. Cast on 37 (41, 45, 49, 53) sts behind worked center sts. Work left sts from holder. There are now 71 (79, 87, 95, 103) sts on needles. Work for 6". Work right 17 (19, 21, 23, 25) sts. BO center 37 (41, 45, 49, 53) sts. Replace with center sts from holder. Cont to work left 17 (19, 21, 23, 25) sts. There are still 71 (79, 87, 95, 103) sts on needles. Cont to measurement C.

2. Change to CC. Beg front neck shaping: Work first row in K1, P1 Rib patt. Work across 28 (31, 34, 37, 40) sts, move center 15 (17, 19, 21, 23) sts to holder, join second ball of yarn, finish row. Working both sides at same time, dec 1 st at each neck edge next 4 RS rows. In row 11, BO all sts at each side with firm tension.

3. On right vertical edge of kangaroo pocket, pick up 23 sts in CC. Work in K1, P1 Rib patt for 1". BO with firm tension. Rep on left side.

Sew top and bottom edges of ribbing to sweater front. On WS of sweater front, sew top and bottom edges of pocket in place. Note that sweater front is ½" taller than pocket.

Collar

1. Put a permanent seam in one shoulder.

2. In CC, PU collar sts as follows: 3 sts from back side neck, 21 (23, 25, 27, 29) sts from back holder, 3 sts from back side neck, 9 sts from front side neck, 15 (17, 19, 21, 23) sts from front holder, 10 sts from front side neck—61 (65, 69, 73, 77) sts.

3. Work in (K1, P1) rib for 7" (or desired length). K1, P1 Rib patt BO with very loose tension. For a turtleneck, remember that the side that starts out on the inside of the sweater body will fold over and become the RS of the turtleneck.

4. Put a permanent seam in the second shoulder, including collar. Reinforce shoulder seams if desired.

Sleeves

1. For each sleeve, with CC, CO 29 (31, 33, 35, 39) sts. Work in K1, P1 Rib patt for 6". Inc 16 sts in last row evenly spaced—45 (47, 49, 51, 55) sts.

2. Join MC and work in Plaid Stitch, inc 1 st at each side 9 (10, 11, 13, 15) times, evenly spaced between top of cuff and measurement F—63 (67, 71, 77, 85) sts.

3. Switch to CC and work in K1, P1 Rib patt for 2". BO with moderate tension.

And Finally

1. Sew in sleeves.

2. Sew side seams and sleeve seams.

Autumn Cardigan

This sweater can be made in gauges of 10–15 stitches = 4" (chunky range).

Model sweater knit in Artfibers Shroom (100% wool; 50 g, 66 yds per skein) and Trendsetter Yarns Dune (41% mohair, 30% acrylic, 12% rayon, 11% nylon, 6% metal; 50 g, 90 yds per skein) on #10½ needles.

Model gauge: 12 sts and 24 rows = 4" in patt

As shown in the model sweater, a combination of exotic yarns can create a classic look. The main yarn is a chunky thick/thin wool. You can see the interesting texture created, especially in the bands. The contrasting yarn is a metallic mohair blend, which is very dressy on its own, but relaxed in combination with the solid black. This works well with yarns that may be too overpowering (or too expensive!) to use on their own. For a similar look without the glitter, try a couple of complementary wool yarns. Or, for something in between, try the shine of a rayon ribbon. If you're showing off a great texture of a yarn like French Braid, try knitting your contrast yarn on both right and wrong side rows.

RIGHT

Sample knit in GGH Goa (50% cotton, 50% acrylic; 50 g, 60 m per skein) and Great Adirondack Yarn Co. French Braid (100% rayon; 100 g, 72 yds per skein) on #10½ needles.

Sample gauge: 14 sts and 24 rows = 4" in patt

Yarn Required (in yards)

Finished Sweater Size	33"	36"	40"	44"	48"
Gauge (No. sts = 4")			Yards		
10			725 MC	775 MC	850 MC
			325 CC	350 CC	400 CC
11		700 MC	800 MC	875 MC	950 MC
		300 CC	350 CC	400 CC	425 CC
12	700 MC	775 MC	875 MC	950 MC	1,050 MC
	300 CC	325 CC	400 CC	425 CC	475 CC
13	750 MC	850 MC	975 MC	1,050 MC	
	325 CC	350 CC	425 CC	475 CC	
14	825 MC	975 MC	975 MC	1,125 MC	
	350 CC	425 CC	425 CC	500 CC	
15	900 MC	975 MC	1,150 MC		
	375 CC	425 CC	500 CC		

Additional Materials

✦ Needles, the size used for gauge swatch

✦ Long, circular needles for button band, the size used for gauge swatch

✦ 5 buttons (or number desired)

Sample knit with two strands of Classic Elite Yarns
Waterspun (felted 100% merino wool; 50 g,
138 yds per skein) and one strand of Manos del
Uruguay Handspun Pure Wool (100% wool;
100 g, 138 yds per skein) on #10½ needles.
Sample gauge: 11 sts and 18 rows = 4" in patt

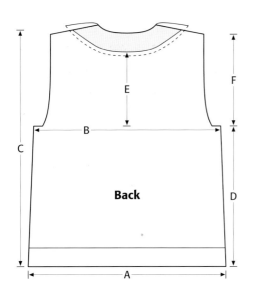

Before You Begin:

1. Make a gauge swatch in MC and CC in the Brick Stitch pattern. This sweater can be made in gauges of 10–15 stitches = 4" (chunky range).

2. Determine the sweater size that you want to make (see page 10).

3. Identify the pattern number that will produce the sweater size that you want (see pages 10–12). Directions are given for pattern number 1; changes for pattern numbers 2, 3, 4, and 5 are in parentheses. Note that a pattern number 1 does not necessarily mean a 33" sweater size!

4. Review the sweater measurements in the table on facing page. The letters in the table correspond to the letters on the diagrams. Adjust lengths as necessary for the fit that you want.

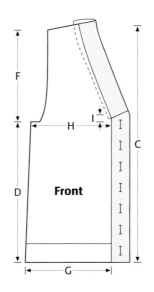

Collar is added later and folded over.

Button bands and collar are added
later. Collar is folded over
from V-neck to shoulder.

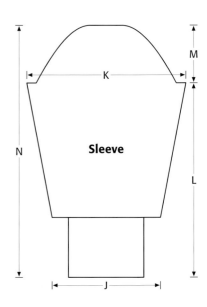

Cuff is to be folded.

Sweater Measurements (in inches)

Finished Sweater Size	33	36	40	44	48
A. Back width at bottom	18	19½	21½	23½	25½
B. Back width at bust	16½	18	20	22	24
C. Back length, front length	22½	24	25½	26	26½
D. Length to armhole	14	15	16	16	16
E. Length from armhole to back neck	7½	8	8½	9	9½
F. Length from armhole to shoulder	8	8½	9	9½	10
G. Front width at bottom (not including button band)	8½	8½	10	11	12½
H. Front width at bust (not including button band)	7½	7½	9	10	11½
I. Length from armhole to front neck	1	1	1	1	1
J. Sleeve width above cuff	10	10	12	12	13
K. Sleeve width at underarm	14	16	17	18	19
L. Sleeve length to underarm	18½	19	20	20	20
M. Length of sleeve cap	5	5½	6	6½	6½
N. Total sleeve length	23½	24½	26	26½	26½

Back

1. With MC, CO 55 (59, 67, 71, 79) sts. Work in K1, P1 Rib patt for 2". Join CC and work in Brick Stitch, dec 1 st each side 2 times between bottom and measurement D—51 (55, 63, 67, 75) sts.

2. At measurement D, beg armhole shaping: BO 2 (2, 3, 3, 3) sts at beg of next 2 rows. Dec 1 st at each side next 2 (2, 3, 3, 3) RS rows—43 (47, 51, 55, 63) sts.

3. At measurement E, beg back neck shaping: Work across 9 (9, 11, 13, 15) sts, join second ball of yarn, BO center 25 (29, 29, 29, 33) sts, finish row. Working both sides at same time, dec 1 st at each neck edge next RS row.

4. AT SAME TIME, at measurement F, beg shoulder shaping: At each shoulder edge, BO 4 (4, 5, 6, 7) sts; 2 rows later, BO rem 4 (4, 5, 6, 7) sts.

Front

1. For each front, with MC, CO 27 (27, 31, 35, 39) sts. Work in K1, P1 Rib patt for 2". Join CC and work in Brick Stitch, dec 1 st at outside edge 2 times between bottom and measurement D—25 (25, 29, 33, 37) sts rem.

2. At measurement D, work armhole shaping as for back—21 (21, 23, 27, 31) sts rem.

3. At measurement I, beg front neck shaping: Dec 1 st at each neck edge 13 (13, 13, 15, 17) times, evenly spaced between measurement I and shoulder—8 (8, 10, 12, 14) sts.

4. AT SAME TIME, at measurement F, work shoulder shaping as for back.

Button Band and Collar

1. Measure st-per-inch gauge for K1, P1 rib border on back piece. Measure length of button band/neck band beg at lower front, up to shoulder, around back neck, and down to lower back. (This measurement should be 55"–70" depending on the size of your sweater). Multiply by rib gauge. With long circular needle and MC, PU approx this number of sts, ending with an odd number. On front and back mark sts that are even with beg of V-neck shaping. Work in K1, P1 Rib patt for 1". Mark locations for buttonholes, with top buttonhole approx ½" below V-neck st and bottom buttonhole centered in hip band (see "Buttonholes," page 135). Make buttonholes. Work band to 2". At beg of next row, BO all sts below V-neck, using a tension that keeps band flat. Work rem sts in row. At beg of next row, BO all sts below V-neck on other front side. Cont to work rem collar sts to 6". BO loosely so collar spreads out to full size.

2. Sew permanent shoulder seams.

Sleeves

1. For each sleeve, with MC, CO 21 (21, 25, 25, 29) sts with very loose tension. Work in K1, P1 Rib patt for 6". Inc 10 sts evenly spaced across last row of rib—31 (31, 35, 35, 39) sts.

2. Join CC and work in Brick Stitch, inc 6 (8, 8, 9, 9) sts at each side evenly spaced between top of cuff and measurement L—43 (47, 51, 53, 57) sts.

3. At measurement L, beg sleeve cap: BO 3 (3, 3, 4, 4) sts at beg of next 2 rows. Dec 1 st at each side of every other RS row until sleeve cap measures 4½ (4½, 4½, 5½, 5½)". BO 2 sts at beg of each row until sleeve cap reaches measurement M. BO rem sts.

And Finally

1. Sew in sleeves.
2. Sew side seams and sleeve seams.
3. Sew on buttons.

Knitting Abbreviations

approx	approximately		**P3tog**	purl 3 stitches together (2-stitch decrease)
beg	begin(ning)		**patt**	pattern
BO	bind off		**PM**	place marker on needle
CC	contrasting color		**psso**	pass slipped stitch(es) over
cn	cable needle		**PU**	pick up
CO	cast on		**pw**	purlwise
cont	continue		**rem**	remaining
dec(s)	decrease(s)		**rep**	repeat
foll	following		**RS**	right side (as opposed to wrong side)
g	grams			
inc(s)	increase(s)		**sl**	slip
K	knit		**SSK**	slip, slip, knit the 2 slipped stitches together (1-stitch decrease)
K1tbl	knit 1 stitch through back loop			
K2tog	knit 2 stitches together (1-stitch decrease)		**SKP**	slip 1 knitwise, K1, pass slipped stitch over (1-stitch decrease)
K3tog	knit 3 stitches together (2-stitch decrease)		**st(s)**	stitch(es)
KS	knit selvage (knit on RS and WS rows)		**St st**	stockinette stitch (knit on RS rows, purl on WS rows)
kw	knitwise		**tog**	together
M1	make 1 stitch (see page 133)		**wyib**	with yarn in back
MC	main color		**WS**	wrong side
oz	ounces		**yds**	yards
P	purl		**YO**	yarn over
P2tog	purl 2 stitches together (1-stitch decrease)			

Yarn Conversion Chart

Yards x .91 = meters

Meters x 1.09 = yards

Grams ÷ 28.35 = ounces

Ounces x 28.35 = grams

Knitting Techniques

*I*n knitting, there are many ways to do everything: cast on, bind off, increase, and decrease. Below is a description of basic techniques that will work well for the sweaters in this book. You may want to explore other techniques to get a different look, more stretch, or better fit with an unusual yarn. If so, look through some of the great instruction books available at your local knitting shop, bookstore, or library.

All of the references in this section assume that the knitter is right-handed. I apologize to all the left-handed knitters!

Cast On (CO)

The cable cast on is a good, all-purpose cast-on method. It's simple, looks neat, and has a nice amount of give.

1. Begin with a slipknot on your left-hand needle. That is stitch number one.

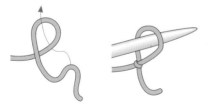

2. Insert the tip of the right-hand needle through the first stitch. Wrap the needle in back of work and pull this yarn to the front. Place this loop on the left-hand needle. That is stitch number two. For all subsequent stitches, insert the right

needle between the two previous stitches on the left needle. Wrap in back, pull the stitch to the front, and place it on the needle.

Insert needle between two stitches. Knit a stitch.

Place new stitch on left needle.

Tip

Most knitters work this cast on as described with two knitting needles. Try using a crochet hook rather than the right-hand knitting needle. It's a better tool for the job!

Getting the right tension in the cast-on row is important. Unfortunately, you can't tell if the cast-on row is too tight or too loose until you have worked a couple of rows. The gauge swatch is the place to work this out. As you admire your swatch, think about whether the cast-on row has enough give for the bottom of the sweater, and perhaps more importantly, enough give for the sleeve cuff. If the cast-on row is too tight, try casting on with larger needles. Once the tension is right on your gauge swatch, use the same technique and needle size when you cast on stitches for your sweater pieces.

Bind Off (BO)

Like casting on, there are several methods available for binding off. The following is the most common method.

To bind off a group of stitches, work the first two stitches in pattern. Pass the first stitch over the second stitch and off the needle. Work the next stitch in pattern and repeat until you have eliminated the desired number of stitches. When you are binding off all remaining stitches on the needle, knit the last two stitches together. This will keep the bind-off row from extending past the side edge of your fabric.

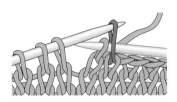

On a shoulder, neck, or sleeve cap, where you are binding off in two or more consecutive right-side rows (or two or more consecutive wrong-side rows), work the first bind-off row as described above. For subsequent bind-off rows, slip the first stitch onto the right needle without working it. This will create more of a diagonal line and less of a stairstep on your edge.

Be very careful about the tension of the bind-off row. Work to a *firm tension with little horizontal stretch* for shoulder edges and cardigan necklines. Work to a *tension that keeps the edge firm and flat* for button bands, neckbands, and open collars. Work to a *loose tension that gives the fabric a little give* for armholes and sleeve caps. Work *very loosely, with lots of horizontal stretch* for turtlenecks and crew necks. To get a loose tension, try switching to a larger needle when you bind off.

Tightening a Bind-Off Row

Once a bind-off row is complete, it can't be loosened (you'll need to redo it if it's too tight), but it can be tightened. To tighten a bind-off row, start at the second stitch. Using your fingernails, pull gently on the front of the loop. This should firm up the *previous* stitch. Continue down the line, taking a little slack out of each stitch. You may be surprised at how much yarn you'll be working with after a few stitches—it's best to tighten a small amount all the way to the end and repeat if necessary. For a very long row (like a cardigan neckline), check the tension of the bind-off row often as you're working.

Increases

Some techniques for increasing the number of stitches will create lacy holes in the work. Some do not. Here's one of each.

Make 1 Stitch (M1)

This is a good all-purpose increase that creates a new stitch *between* two existing stitches without creating a hole in the work. Work to the point where you want to make a stitch. With the left-hand needle, reach behind the work and lift the horizontal yarn that connects the last stitch on the right needle and the first stitch on the left needle. Knit this new stitch through the front loop to twist it closed (otherwise there *will* be a hole in the work that looks like a yarn over).

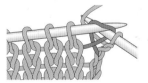

Insert left needle from back to front through "running thread."   Knit into front of stitch.

Yarn Over (YO)

Sometimes you *want* a hole. A yarn over creates a new stitch and makes a hole in the work. To work, wrap the yarn around the right needle between two stitches. In subsequent rows, treat this extra loop of yarn as a stitch.

The way the needle is wrapped depends on the type of stitches on either side of the yarn over.

- Between two knit stitches, pull the working yarn forward between the needles and over the top of the right needle, leaving the yarn in back. Knit the next stitch normally.

- Between a knit and a purl stitch, or between two purl stitches, pull the yarn to the front (as to purl) and wrap once completely around the right needle, leaving the yarn in front. Purl the next stitch normally.

- Between a purl and a knit stitch, leave the yarn in front after the purl stitch. As you knit the second stitch, let the yarn wrap around the right needle.

Decreases

All decreases in this book are meant to be worked on the right side of the work. There are three types of decreases. Take a minute to get this right—it really will look funny if you use the wrong decrease!

- For decreases worked on purl stitches, simply purl two stitches together (P2tog). To work, insert the right needle purlwise into both the first and second stitch on the left needle. Wrap the right needle purlwise and pull the new stitch through the two old stitches. Note that decreases on purl stitches do not slant.

- Decreases that slant up to the left include armhole shaping on right-hand side of front or back piece, right-hand side of sleeve cap, left-hand side of front or back neck shaping, and decreases in left half of Cascading Leaf pattern. To work, slip one stitch as if to knit, knit the following stitch, pass the slipped stitch over the worked stitch and off the needle. This is abbreviated sl 1, K1, psso, or SKP.

- Decreases that slant up to the right include armhole shaping on left-hand edge of the front or back piece, left-hand side of sleeve cap, right-hand side of front or back neck shaping, and decreases in right half of Cascading Leaf

pattern. To work, knit two stitches together (K2tog) as follows: Insert the right needle knitwise into the second stitch and the first stitch on the left needle. Wrap the right needle knitwise and pull the new stitch through the two old stitches.

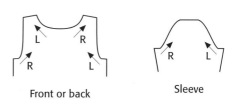

Front or back   Sleeve

R   Decreases that slant up to the right
L   Decreases that slant up to the left

Spacing Increases and Decreases

If you have several increases or decreases to work within a row, they should usually be spaced evenly across the row. Mentally divide the row into as many equal-size pieces as you have increases/ decreases to work. Work one increase/decrease in the middle of each segment.

In shaping necklines and sleeves, you often have several increases or decreases to work over a given length of fabric. To determine the right spacing, start with your row gauge—the number of rows worked over 4". Divide this number by eight to get the number of right-side rows per inch. Multiply by the length (in inches) over which you're increasing/decreasing. This is the number of right-side rows available for increasing/decreasing. Distribute the increases/decreases you need evenly over the right-side rows available.

- Once in a blue moon, you will be lucky and the numbers will work out evenly. For example, say you'll need 10 increases in 20 right-side rows; you can increase in every other right-side row. More often, you'll have numbers that don't divide evenly. For example, five increases in 13 right-side rows. Don't worry about being overly precise in the spacing. As long as the increases/decreases aren't all clumped together, the line of the fabric will be fine. In this example, you might choose rows 2, 5, 7, 10, and 12 to work the increases.

✦ In the unlikely event that you need more increases/decreases than there are right-side rows, work increases/decreases in all of the right-side rows and as many wrong-side rows as necessary.

✦ If the number of increases/decreases is almost as large as the number of right-side rows, it may be easier to think about the rows in which you *don't* work an increase or decrease, spacing them evenly over the given length.

Short Rows

With short rows, some stitches on the needle are worked while others are not. When short rows are worked on one edge of a narrow band, this will create a curve by making one edge longer than the other. Short rows are typically worked in pairs. If they are worked on the right-hand edge of the fabric, there will be a right-side row followed by a wrong-side row. If the short rows are needed on the left-hand edge of the fabric, there will be a wrong-side row followed by a right-side row. When working short rows, a hole will form unless the worked stitches are linked to the unworked stitches. This is done by wrapping the next stitch before you turn the work.

For a pair of short rows, begin by working the specified number of stitches in the first row. With the yarn in back of the work, slip the next stitch from the left needle to the right. Move the yarn to the front and slip the same stitch back to the left needle. This stitch is now "wrapped." Turn the work and work back to the edge stitch. In the next full row, treat the wrapped stitch as follows:

✦ If the wrapped stitch appears as a purl stitch *when viewed from the right side of the work,* work it normally.

✦ If the wrapped stitch appears as a knit stitch *when viewed from the right side of the work,* work up to the wrapped stitch. With the right-hand needle, pick up the wrapped yarn and place it on the left needle. Work the next stitch by picking up the wrap and the stitch together.

Buttonholes

This technique will make a complete buttonhole in a single row of work. As described, this buttonhole will be the width of three stitches, with a little extra stretch. For a narrower or wider buttonhole, adjust the numbers accordingly.

1. Work to the position of the buttonhole, bring the yarn to the front, slip the next stitch purlwise, and then return the yarn to the back.

2. *Slip the next stitch; then on right-hand needle, pass the second stitch over the end stitch and drop it off the needle. Repeat from * two times. Slip the last bound-off stitch to the left needle and turn work.

3. Move the yarn to the back and use the cable cast on to cast on four stitches (see "Cast On," page 132). Turn work.

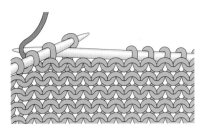

4. With yarn in back, slip first stitch from left needle and pass extra cast-on stitch over it to close buttonhole. Work to end of row.

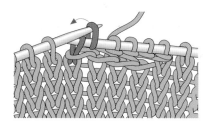

Sometimes, a small gap will appear on each side of the buttonhole. To tidy this up, on the next right-side row, twist the pair of stitches on either side of the three buttonhole stitches. Use a front twist for the stitches on the right, and a back twist for the stitches on the left. Using a cable needle, for a front twist, hold this stitch at the front of the work; for a back twist, hold this stitch to the back of the work and work the next stitch from the left needle, work stitch from cable needle.

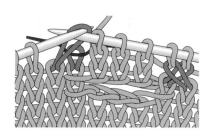

Blocking

If your pieces need blocking, I recommend doing it before seaming the pieces together. Find a flat surface that you can stick pins into. If you don't have a special blocking form, try a mattress, a padded table cover, or a few thicknesses of towels or linens. Lay the sweater pieces out flat, right sides up. Pin the edges down using straight pins or T-pins inserted at an angle. Make sure the pieces, as pinned, are in the final measurements you want them to have. Lay a damp towel over the pinned pieces.

Check the yarn label for warnings about heat and steam. If your fibers are delicate or metallic, press the damp towel down lightly with your hands, transferring some moisture to the knitted pieces.

If your yarn can take some steam, place a warm iron above the towel to steam the knitted pieces. *Do not put the weight of the iron on the pieces.* This would flatten the texture you've worked so hard to create.

Remove the towel, and leave the knitted pieces pinned in place until they are completely dry.

Seams

Different seams require different techniques. The shoulder seam needs to be firm. Because of the way the stitches meet at the shoulder, it is generally easy to create an invisible seam that looks like another row of knitting. Vertical seams, which include side seams, sleeve seams, and raglan armhole seams, need some give and can also be made invisible. For bulky yarns, use flat, vertical seams for the smoothest look. Armhole seams require a combination of techniques.

Shoulder Seams

Place front and back pieces face up on a table with the bound-off shoulder stitches lined up. Using the same yarn as for knitting (the tail from binding off or a fresh piece) and a tapestry needle, bring the needle up through the center of a stitch at the edge of one piece. On the other piece, pick up two strands of yarn, inserting the needle in the space between stitches. Going back to the first piece, pick up two strands of yarn inserting the needle into the center of a stitch. For each stitch, insert the needle in the space where the last stitch on that piece came out.

Adjust the tension so the sewn stitches are the

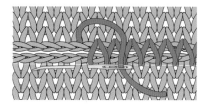

same size as the knitted stitches. This seam should look like an extra row of knitting on top of the bound-off shoulder stitches.

Armhole Seams

On a knitted sweater, the armhole seam is generally sewn after the shoulder seam and before the side seam and sleeve seam. Place the sweater, right side up, on a flat surface with the armhole facing you. Place the sleeve, right side up, so the center of the sleeve cap lines up with the shoulder seam. The outside edge of the sleeve cap must be at least as long as the edge of the armhole—it will usually be one or two inches longer. (If it's not, you will need to reknit the sleeve with more width or a taller cap [see pages 16–18]. With safety pins, join the pieces together at the center cap. Pin them together at the far edges, lining up the bound-off stitches at the armhole and the beginning of the sleeve cap. Pin the pieces together every two to three inches, distributing the extra length of the sleeve cap evenly.

Begin the seam at the shoulder and work out. Use the remaining tail from sewing or reinforcing the shoulder seam or a fresh piece of yarn with a tapestry needle. The seam should run between the selvage stitch and the second stitch along the armhole of the sweater front and back. Pick up two vertical bars of yarn with each stitch. Along the sleeve cap, insert the needle into the center of the stitches or in the space between stitches. Always try to pick up two or three strands of yarn with each stitch, and stay two strands from the outside of the sleeve cap. Adjust the length of the stitch as necessary to keep the two pieces aligned.

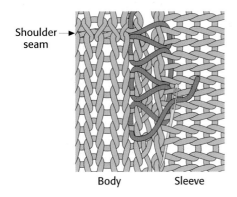

Shoulder seam →

Body   Sleeve

Vertical Seams

Place the two pieces being joined next to each other, right sides up, on a flat surface. Side seams and sleeve seams are worked from the bottom to the armhole. Using the same yarn used for knitting and a tapestry needle, begin with a loop (or a figure eight) that connects the cast-on rows of the two pieces. The seam should run between the selvage stitch and the second stitch. For the first seam stitch, pick up a single horizontal bar of yarn. For each subsequent stitch, insert the needle where the last stitch on that side came out and pick up the next two horizontal bars of yarn. Alternate sides. Keep the sewing yarn quite loose—there should be as much give in the seam as there is in the knitted fabric. Check often to make sure your seam will stretch vertically. Loosen your stitches if necessary. Also check that your pieces remain aligned vertically. Adjust your seam stitch by picking up one bar or three bars, as necessary, to realign.

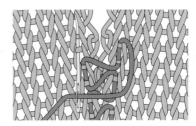

Weaving Side Seam

Flat Seams (Chain-Stitch Seams)

In a flat seam, the two pieces are joined together with a loose chain stitch worked right into the knots of the selvage. It lies completely flat, creating no bulk inside the sweater. I use this stitch with very bulky yarns, where the volume of a single stitch on the inside can change the fit (especially on a sleeve). There is no seam allowance; that is, no portion of the knitted piece is lost in the seam. In fact, the chain will add slightly to the size of the sweater. This is usually helpful on chunky or super-chunky fabrics. In this gauge range, losing two stitches at each seam could shrink the sweater by one or two inches! This seam does not work well with more delicate weights of fabric.

Because this seam is visible, always use the same yarn as used in the knitted piece. If there are contrasting bands, change the yarn used for the seam at the edge of the band.

Place the two pieces being joined next to each other, right sides up, on a flat surface. Work from the bottom edge up. Using a tapestry needle and the same yarn used for knitting, join the pieces at the bottom of the seam with a loop of yarn through the first selvage knot on each piece. Pull the tapestry needle up through the middle of this loop. Insert the needle up through the next knot on the left piece and down through the next knot on the right piece. Insert the needle down into the middle of the first loop and come up in the middle of the first chain stitch. For each subsequent "link," insert the needle up through the next knot on the left and down through the next knot on the right. Insert the needle down through the center of the previous link in the chain and up through the current link. Repeat to the end of the seam.

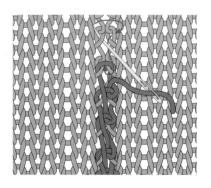

This seam must be worked very loosely! The seam must be able to stretch with the fabric. As you work the seam, stretch it often, and make sure there is a lot of slack in the links of the chain. You should be able to see through the seam as you're working it. When the sweater is worn, gravity will pull the links down and pull the pieces closer together. Note that this seam can be tightened later if necessary, but it can't be loosened. Make it loose!

Reinforcing Seams and Edges

There are a couple areas of a sweater that are prone to stretching. One is the shoulder seams, which carry the weight of the sweater; second, the back neck on a cardigan or V-neck sweater; and maybe the button bands on lightweight fabrics. Reinforcing one or more of these will keep the sweater fitting right.

To reinforce a seam, a second seam is added, using a stitch that doesn't stretch. A common method is to work a row of slip-stitch crochet across the seam. This is worked on the wrong side, with the sweater folded on the seam line. With the yarn in back, *insert a crochet hook through both thicknesses of fabric in the same spaces used in the seam. Wrap yarn around the hook and pull the loop through the stitch and the loop on the hook. Insert the crochet hook again one or two knit stitches to the left, and repeat from * for the length of the seam.

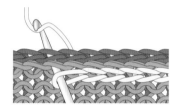

The neckbands in Elegant Cardigan and Easy Cardigan are ribbed vertically from the bottom up and meet at the center back. You can easily reinforce these neckbands with a row of slip-stitch crochet. Working from the right side of the fabric with the yarn behind the work, insert the crochet hook into the center of a knit stitch. Work as described above, except insert the crochet hook again in the same column of stitches one or two rows later. In a stockinette stitch or the knit stitch of a rib, these stitches are nearly invisible. Make sure your chain stitches are the right length to match the band.

Another stitch that works well to reinforce a buttonhole or a seam is a buttonhole stitch, worked with a tapestry needle. Work this stitch around a buttonhole to make it more firm and/or a little smaller. To reinforce a seam, work it on the inside of the sweater, capturing the seam allowance with the stitch.

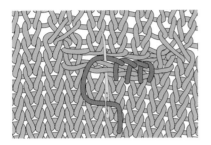

Pick-Up-and-Knit Bands

Many sweaters are finished with pick-up-and-knit neckbands, button and buttonhole bands, armbands and/or collars. They are often worked in a different stitch, and sometimes a different yarn, than the body of the sweater. For most bands, you need to calculate the number of stitches to pick up. You'll need to make a gauge swatch for the band first. It should be about 5" wide and as many rows as the band will be when bound off. To determine the stitch gauge of the band, measure the number of stitches worked over 4" and then divide by 4. This is your stitch-per-inch trim gauge. The number of stitches to pick up for the band is the length of the band (in inches) times the stitch-per-inch trim gauge.

Distribute the picked-up stitches evenly across the length of the band. You may want to divide the pick-up edge with markers into equal-length sections (four or more) and pick up the same number of stitches in each section.

To pick up stitches, I recommend using a crochet hook and a circular needle if the band is curved. If the band is very long, you'll need a long circular needle to hold all the stitches. (Lengths up to approximately 36" are commonly available.) Lay the sweater flat with the right side up, and let the needle fall along the pick-up edge. With the yarn in back of the work, reach through the fabric with the crochet hook to pull up a loop of yarn. Place this loop on the needle. Make sure the first and last picked-up stitches are as close to the beginning and end of your edge as possible.

For vertical pick-up edges, insert the crochet hook in the space between the selvage stitch and the second stitch. Try to leave two or three horizontal bars of yarn between new stitches. For horizontal edges, pull new stitches through existing stitches (one new stitch through every existing stitch unless your trim gauge is quite different than your sweater gauge). For curves, you need to be a little creative. Whenever possible, pull a new stitch through existing stitches. If you need to use the spaces between stitches, try to find tight spaces rather than loose spaces; the loose spaces may create holes. If you put the new stitches onto a circular needle, you can easily see how smooth your curve will be. Redo any picked-up stitches that throw off the line of the curve. *It is more important to have a smooth line than to have the exact number of stitches.*

Work your band/collar in the pattern indicated, *including selvage stitches.* You can increase or decrease picked-up stitches in the first row if you need to adjust the number of stitches, such as to get an odd number of stitches for seed stitch. Note that neckbands and armbands require a substantial number of decreases in progressive rows to lie flat. For example, a 1"-wide armband with a pick-up edge 27" long has a finished edge of only 22"; the last row is 5" shorter than the first row! Work all decreases as specified, usually concentrated in the most sharply curved portion of the band.

The tension of the bind-off row is critical to the success of the band. Armbands, neckbands, and button bands should be quite firm. I recommend that you bind them off initially with moderate tension and then tighten as necessary to get a smooth fit. Collars generally need to be bound off much more loosely so they can spread out fully.

Crocheted Edges

Crocheted edges are a quick and attractive way to finish the edges of your knitted pieces. A single crochet edge will add very little width (perhaps a half inch, depending on your yarn). For more width—to add a little more coverage at the armhole for instance—try two rows of single crochet or a double-crochet edge. Shell edging will also add a decorative finish. Consider a contrasting yarn for the crocheted edge, such as a solid yarn to contrast with a variegated pattern, or a smooth yarn for a comfortable finish on a rough or scratchy yarn.

For any of these crocheted edges, experiment to find the correct spacing of crocheted stitches on horizontal stretches, vertical stretches, and curves. There are no right answers here; it will depend on the yarns used, the knitted-fabric stitch, and the size of your crochet stitch. Generally, you want the crocheted edge to lie flat and straight. On curved necklines and armholes, you may want the crocheted edge to pull the curve in slightly. In that case, space the stitches a little farther apart. Around corners (such as the front neck of a cardigan), you'll need extra crochet stitches. Try working two or three stitches in the same spot at the corner.

Crocheted edges are worked on the right side of the sweater, from right to left. Begin your crocheted edge at an inconspicuous point. Using any stitch described below, insert the crochet hook into a knitted stitch or in the space between stitches. As you work stitches, try to leave at least two strands of knitted yarn between your crochet stitches. Also try to insert your crochet hook at least 2 strands from the edge of the knitted fabric. To join the first crochet stitch to the last, crochet to within the width of one stitch to your first stitch.

Cut the crochet yarn about 12" long. Pull the end of the yarn out of the last stitch; there will be one long strand coming from this stitch. With a tapestry needle, loop this yarn through the first stitch and reinsert it into the last stitch.

Single Crochet (sc)

To start, insert the crochet hook through a space in the knitted fabric. Draw a loop of yarn from the back to the right side. Reaching over the edge of the fabric with the crochet hook, draw another loop of yarn and pull it through the loop on the hook. For each subsequent stitch, insert the hook in a space to the left and draw a loop through to the front of the fabric (two loops on hook). Wrap yarn around the hook and pull it through the two loops already on the hook (one loop left on hook). Repeat as needed across the edge of the knitted fabric.

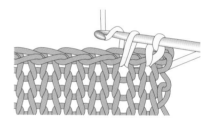

Insert hook into stitch, yarn over hook,
pull loop through to front, yarn over hook.

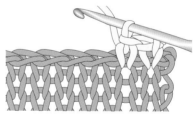

Pull loop through both loops on hook.

Double Crochet (dc)

Begin as single crochet (one loop on hook). For each stitch, wrap yarn around the hook and insert it through the fabric and draw up the loop (three loops on hook). Wrap yarn around the hook and draw it through two loops on the hook (two loops on hook). Wrap again and draw the yarn through two loops on hook (one loop on hook).

 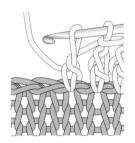

Yarn over hook, insert hook into stitch, yarn over hook, pull through to front.

Yarn over hook, pull through two loops on hook.

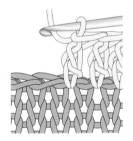

Yarn over hook, pull through remaining two loops on hook.

Shell Edging

Begin as single crochet (one loop on hook). In a space ½" to ¾" to the left, work five double crochets *in the same space*. Work one single crochet in a space ½" to ¾" to the left of the five double crochets. Alternate the single crochet and the five double crochets across the edge. Getting the right distance between stitches is the key to this stitch. Increase or decrease the distance as necessary to get the right look.

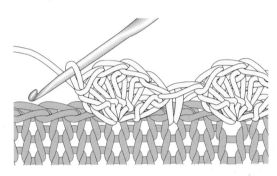

Resources

All of the materials used in this book were purchased from retail sources over the last year or two (or four!). A few of the yarns here were purchased in the "marketplace" of locally held knitting conventions. If you've never been to a convention, I recommend them highly. Many classes are offered on a wide variety of knitting topics, and the marketplace presents dozens of great yarn stores all under one roof. In particular, I like to look for the cottage industries—artisans that work in small quantities to produce some really special yarns. And don't forget to shop for buttons!

Many of the yarns in this book were purchased from Artfibers, a wonderful yarn source located in downtown San Francisco. Artfibers produces all of their yarns, and the selection changes frequently. The yarns shown here may no longer be available, but I bet you'll find something similar—or something completely different that knocks your socks off! See their current selection at www.Artfibers.com.

Most of the remaining yarns were purchased at a wonderful shop, Fengari, in Half Moon Bay, California. There is an incredible selection of yarns out on the floor and even more hiding in the back room and in other mysterious locations. Check with owners Ann Gevas and Kim McFall if you're looking for something in particular.

Almost all of the buttons used in this book are from Britex Fabrics in downtown San Francisco. The trip to the fourth floor is worth it—the button selection is enormous and the staff has an amazing knack for finding just the right button.

These are some of the great shops in my area. For something new, explore the stores near where you live, work, and travel! Yarn shops are popping up everywhere, and there are lots of mail-order and Internet sources. For great buttons, try stores that specialize in handcrafts, antiques, and vintage clothing.

Bibliography

Stanfield, Lesley. *The New Knitting Stitch Library.* London: Quarto Publishing, 1992 (published in United States by Lark Books, Asheville, N.C. , 1998).

The Harmony Guides: 440 More Knitting Stitches, Volume 3. London: Collins &

Brown, 1998 (first published by Lyric Books in 1987 as the *Harmony Guide to Knitting Stitches,* Volume 2).

Vogue Knitting. New York: Pantheon Books, 1989.

new and bestselling titles from

America's Best-Loved Craft & Hobby Books®
America's Best-Loved Knitting Books®

America's Best-Loved Quilt Books®

NEW RELEASES
Beaded Elegance
Beyond Wool
Burgoyne Surrounded
Clever Quarters
Coffee-Time Quilts
Collage Cards
Crocheted Lace
Dutch Treat
Endless Stars
English Cottage Quilts
Fast-Forward Your Quilting
Garden Stroll, A
Holidays at Home
Knit It Now!
Knits from the Heart
Little Box of Scarves, The
Little Box of Sweaters, The
Machine-Embroidered Quilts
Mad about Plaid!
Quilter's Quick Reference Guide, The
Romantic Quilts
Sensational Settings, Revised Edition
Simple Blessings
Stack a New Deck
Star-Studded Quilts
Stitch and Split Appliqué
Warm Up to Wool
Year of Cats…in Hats!, A

APPLIQUÉ
Appliquilt in the Cabin
Artful Album Quilts
Blossoms in Winter
Garden Party
Shadow Appliqué
Sunbonnet Sue All through the Year

HOLIDAY QUILTS & CRAFTS
Christmas Cats and Dogs
Christmas Delights
Creepy Crafty Halloween
Handcrafted Christmas, A
Hocus Pocus!
Make Room for Christmas Quilts
Welcome to the North Pole

LEARNING TO QUILT
101 Fabulous Rotary-Cut Quilts
Casual Quilter, The
Happy Endings, Revised Edition
Loving Stitches, Revised Edition
More Fat Quarter Quilts
Professional Machine Quilting
Simple Joys of Quilting, The
Your First Quilt Book (or it should be!)

PAPER PIECING
40 Bright and Bold Paper-Pieced Blocks
50 Fabulous Paper-Pieced Stars
Down in the Valley
Easy Machine Paper Piecing
For the Birds
Papers for Foundation Piecing
Quilter's Ark, A
Show Me How to Paper Piece
Traditional Quilts to Paper Piece

QUILTS FOR BABIES & CHILDREN
Easy Paper-Pieced Baby Quilts
Even More Quilts for Baby
More Quilts for Baby
Quilts for Baby
Sweet and Simple Baby Quilts

ROTARY CUTTING/SPEED PIECING
101 Fabulous Rotary-Cut Quilts
365 Quilt Blocks a Year Perpetual
    Calendar
1000 Great Quilt Blocks
Around the Block Again
Around the Block with Judy Hopkins
Clever Quilts Encore
Log Cabin Fever
Once More around the Block
Pairing Up
Strips and Strings
Triangle-Free Quilts
Triangle Tricks

SCRAP QUILTS
Nickel Quilts
Rich Traditions
Scrap Frenzy
Spectacular Scraps
Successful Scrap Quilts

TOPICS IN QUILTMAKING
Asian Elegance
Batiks and Beyond
Bed and Breakfast Quilts
Four Seasons of Quilts
Judy Murrah's Jacket Jackpot
Meadowbrook Quilts
Patchwork Memories
Quilter's Home: Winter, The
Snowflake Follies
Split-Diamond Dazzlers
Time to Quilt
World of Quilts, A

CRAFTS
20 Decorated Baskets
ABCs of Making Teddy Bears, The
Blissful Bath, The
Creating with Paint
Handcrafted Garden Accents
Painted Whimsies
Pretty and Posh
Purely Primitive
Sassy Cats
Stamp in Color
Trashformations

KNITTING & CROCHET
365 Knitting Stitches a Year Perpetual
    Calendar
Basically Brilliant Knits
Classic Knitted Vests
Crochet for Tots
Crocheted Aran Sweaters
Crocheted Socks!
Knits for Children and Their Teddies
Knitted Sweaters for Every Season
Knitted Throws and More
Knitter's Template, A
Simply Beautiful Sweaters for Men
Style at Large
Today's Crochet
Too Cute! Cotton Knits for Toddlers
Treasury of Rowan Knits, A
Ultimate Knitter's Guide, The

Our books are available at
bookstores and your favorite
craft, fabric, and yarn retailers.
If you don't see the title
you're looking for, visit us at
www.martingale-pub.com
or contact us at:

1-800-426-3126

International: 1-425-483-3313
Fax: 1-425-486-7596
Email: info@martingale-pub.com

1/04